Penguin Book

Tumbledown

Charles Wood was born in Guernsey in 1932 to theatrical parents, themselves theatrical children. On leaving Birmingham College of Art in 1949 he became a regular soldier for five and a half years. His plays for the theatre include *Cockade* (1963); *Tie Up the Ballcock* (1964), later directed as a film by the author; *Fill the Stage with Happy Hours* (1967); *Dingo* (1967); *H* (1969); *Veterans* (1972); *Jingo* (1975); *Red Star* (1984); *Across from the Garden of Allah* (1986); and *Arabia*. He has written extensively for television. His television adaptation of *My Family and Other Animals* will be seen at the end of 1987. His screenplays include *The Knack* (winner of the Grand Prix, Cannes 1965), *Help!* (1965), *How I Won the War* (1967), *The Charge of the Light Brigade* (1968), *The Long Day's Dying* (1969), *Cuba* (1979), *Wagner* (1983) and *Red Monarch* (1983).

Charles Wood is married with two children and lives in Oxfordshire.

Charles Wood

Tumbledown

a screenplay

PENGUIN BOOKS

PENGUIN BOOKS

Published by the Penguin Group
27 Wrights Lane, London W8 5TZ, England
Viking Penguin Inc., 40 West 23rd Street, New York, New York 10010, USA
Penguin Books Australia Ltd, Ringwood, Victoria, Australia
Penguin Books Canada Ltd, 2801 John Street, Markham, Ontario, Canada L3R 1B4
Penguin Books (NZ) Ltd, 182–190 Wairau Road, Auckland 10, New Zealand

Penguin Books Ltd, Registered Offices: Harmondsworth, Middlesex, England

First published 1987
Reprinted 1988

For permission to reprint extracts from the song
'I Will Go' grateful acknowledgement is made to the
Corries and Lochside Music Ltd.

Made and printed in Great Britain by
Richard Clay Ltd, Bungay, Suffolk
Set in 10/12pt Lasercomp Palatino

For Robert, a remarkable young man

Acknowledgements

My thanks to Mark Burns, who rightly comes first; to John and Jean Lawrence, whom I have come to know and admire; to Mark Mathewson, who was with Robert on Mount Tumbledown; to Richard Broke and to Tim Corrie; but, most of all, to Robert Lawrence, M.C.

Preface

It all started in 1984, when Mark Burns sent me a copy of a *Guardian* article dated Friday, 17 August. The heading was 'Falklands victims the army tried to forget', and the subheading read, 'Seumas Milne meets an officer who was shot in the head in the South Atlantic. He says the sniper who hit him was doing his job but believes the military establishment and Civil Service have not done theirs. He was kept out of the way at the St Paul's service of remembrance, had to pay for a "free" car and was told nothing about how to start a new life.'

It went on: 'Lt Robert Lawrence was a 21-year-old Scots Guards officer with five years' army service when he was sent to the Falklands on the *QE2* in April 1982. A few days before his 22nd birthday and 1½ hours before the Argentinian surrender he was shot in the back of the head by a sniper during the assault on Tumbledown Mountain. For his part in the action, he was awarded the Military Cross.'

In 1986 I wrote the following letter to the *Guardian*:

Sir, Some time ago I wrote a film about the experiences of Robert Lawrence, MC, in the Falklands and after. With him and others I have tried to have my screenplay made into a film and at last the BBC has agreed to a production. The screenplay, *Tumbledown*, was very carefully written with the full co-operation of Robert Lawrence and his family. I avoided any political stance, concentrating on the courage of Robert Lawrence in the Falklands, when recovering from his terrible wound and, not least, when recounting his feelings honestly and accurately. This carefully written film has in the past few days been labelled 'anti-establishment' (*Evening Standard*, 30 September) and the antithesis of the sentiments expressed by [another writer] whose play about the Falklands has been postponed by the BBC. My own attitudes to war and to the Falklands conflict have been quoted as indicative of the attitude of my script. Nothing could be further from the truth, but I fear *Tumbledown* will now bear another label apart from 'left-wing . . . subversive . . . anti-establishment' (*Daily Mail*, 30 September); it will become 'the film the BBC put on instead of The Falklands Play', with all the obvious implications. There is also, in my opinion, a real danger that the

BBC will cancel our film altogether to show its new-broom 'lack of bias', regardless of the fact that I have taken great pains to show no bias whatsoever.

Between the first article and my letter I had met Robert Lawrence, written and rewritten the treatment and screenplay of *Tumbledown* and, with Robert and Mark Burns and others, notably Simon Relph and Alan Wright, attempted to set up the film and failed totally in spite of British Film Year.

When David Puttnam read the treatment for *Tumbledown* he said it ought to be called *The Last Hero*. In 1964 Ken Tynan read a play of mine called *I Don't Hold With Heroes* and suggested I changed the title to *Dingo*, as being less on the nose. Because the National Theatre intended doing the play and in the event were prevented only by the Lord Chamberlain's Guards, the resistance of certain theatre governors and a will-o'-the-wisp director called John Dexter (who never turned up for a meeting) I agreed. *Dingo* it became, but the first title is more indicative of my general attitude to 'heroes'. On the other hand, though David didn't in the end want to make the film in the way we hoped (more of which later), I could see his reason for offering the alternative title. I would add a question mark, *The Last Hero?*, not to show I doubted the conventional heroic qualities of my hero but just because he may *not* be the last unfortunate to bear the designation.

The Lord Chamberlain refused to grant a licence for *Dingo* so that it might be produced by the National Theatre at the Old Vic in 1964. Ken Tynan, who presumably attended the meetings with Lord Olivier and the Guards officer in command of reading plays, told me that *Dingo* was considered subversive. I wasn't surprised to learn this. I had hoped it was, as I hope all my work is – in the way that, for instance, Peter Nichols's *A Day in the Death of Joe Egg* is rightly regarded as subversive. I am not interested in writers who are not subversive. Most dramatists are. Privileged researchers working as dramatic chroniclers are hardly ever.

A controversial play is easier to get on than a film, but I waited three years to see *Dingo* on the stage of the Bristol Arts Centre, and later, less successfully, at the Royal Court. I had to paint and construct and design the set – mostly sand and camouflage nets – and pay for the privilege; royalties from *Dingo* were mortgaged for another few years to come. Without the genius and enthusiasm of the less than wispy director Geoffrey Reeves and actors like Henry Woolf and Tom Kempinski (to name but the short and the long of it), who were prepared to work for nothing, the play would never have been seen. I wish I could cry success, but of course I can't. Nobody wanted to see it, even though subversive. A good many years later *Dingo* was revived by the RSC, filled the theatre occasionally but was hardly considered subversive at all. Nevertheless, had it not been thought subversive at the time, I would have been the first modern dramatist to be produced at the National Theatre.

David Puttnam is not afraid of controversy, and he was not afraid of *Tumbledown*, but he didn't feel it was going to make a feature film. I did; he didn't. I was going to write it as a feature film for myself. Usually I am commissioned to write a film based on a book or a play by someone else. When the idea is original it comes from the producer or director concerned, or I have taken the idea to a director and we have reached a compromise objective. That is perhaps the way it should be, and when I have written for Richard Lester our thoughts have more often than not coincided, but I am prepared to work towards the objective of the director and sometimes enjoy doing so. If I can slip in a few bits of 'woodery-pokery' along the way, so much the better. I felt the urge to please nobody but myself with *Tumbledown*, to get it right for myself and to resist whatever inducements might be offered. None was, though assurances were asked for, like the comment from a producer on the telephone after reading my treatment: 'Charles, promise me it's an anti-war film.'

David Puttnam offered us a television production, possibly in conjunction with Channel Four, and a small budget of something like £300,000.

An extract from a letter from Enigma: 'The Falklands War is an issue which really concerns only the English at the moment.' From a memorandum of a reader at Goldcrest: 'Every once in a while I see material that I find I need to turn down for certain reasons, but which kills me to do so . . . There is a potentially strong story here, but I don't know that it could go as a feature . . . I think the Falklands crisis, and a story concerning it, is terribly parochial. I don't see American audiences flocking to a story about that war . . . But Robert's story is not about war [but] about larger issues . . . Unfortunately, it's also the story of *Coming Home*, *All Quiet on the Western Front*, *Johnny Got His Gun*; I just can't see replaying it.'

As the reader for Goldcrest suspected, there is nothing new in *Tumbledown* (but, of course, it is the way you tell them). The central character is a soldier and hero of Empire – just when we thought it was safe to come out. As Robert says often, what he did down there in the Falklands has made him an outsider, a freak even, as surely as it has crippled him. Brought up in a service family, he was unlikely to question the notions of duty and honour absorbed at home and, later, at Fettes, nor would he meet many dissenters or pay them any regard. Honour and duty are admirable qualities: that they are often spoken of against a background of unspeakable brutality and savagery does nothing to detract from their intrinsic worth. To be a soldier, if the undertaking is fully considered and understood, is a noble vocation. A soldier offers his life, and often it is taken. Nobody is astonished when it is, nor should they be.

It is perhaps true that notions of honour and duty seem to reside most often in the thoughts of young men and women of a particular social grouping. They are only notions, however: true honour and duty can surface anywhere – on the factory floor, in hospital wards, at the coal face, in board rooms, as well as on the deck of a fighting ship or during the stumble of a fighting patrol. It is sad that these notions of honour, duty and service to one's country are considered the quaint and perhaps deceitful presumptions of the privileged because all possessors of such notions, no matter how sincerely they are held, tend to get tarred with the same brush, the same sticky accretion of fast cars, bread rolls and sprouts in flight, true-blue muddy knees, Sloane Square lurching and the *boff de politesse*.

Peter Nichols wrote me a letter after reading *Tumbledown*. He has never been seduced by the wild throbbing of the drums of unreason, honour and duty and can never understand my ambivalence in matters military. He wrote: 'You are an amazing and natural writer of films. The story takes bold leaps and yet wouldn't, I think, ever be confusing. The way you keep the best (or worse) for last is very brave and strong. You're right to try to hold on to it and not let some mindless berk make it into a video nasty . . .'

Eventually, after help from Simon Relph and Alan Wright and the National Film Development Fund, we looked as if we were getting somewhere, the main part of the money coming from Rank perhaps. But now we came upon the stumbling block of the American distributor. Without a deal with an American distributor, Rank had no interest in putting up anything. The Americans were not interested unless we came up with an overtly anti-war film or a Rambo-style kick-the-spics-for-a-shit film. Peter Nichols wrote: 'The trouble for me is that, feeling as I do about war, I can't really sympathize ... It was the first mention of heroism [in the script] that opened the door to my old quasi-pacifism. I'm only an impure peacenik because I see in a wishy-washy way that there may be good wars. May. And to be avoided by any means we can. Of course you've never said simple things about war, which is why you can write so much about it and I can't. You believe we can't understand war without understanding the warmakers and this springs in you from an admiration for their discipline and a love of their ethic ... Come to think of it I've probably responded just as you meant me to, with my own kind of rage at the whole bloody mess. So apart from your artistic success you've had a propaganda victory too, though I wish I weren't so worried about your own love for these men and their larks.'

An accepted fact is that it is enough to die in battle to become a hero: the slate is wiped clean. In *Dingo*, when a character called Tanky has been persuaded to attempt an escape by a bullying, jumped-up, self-promoted NCO and then killed on the wire of his POW camp, the following dialogue takes place between the departing Dingo and the dangling corpse of Tanky:

DINGO: Hey, hey, come on, Tanky. You're a hero, having died.

TANKY: I don't hold with bleeding heroes.

DINGO: No, no, look out there, I've told you before, out there (*indicates audience*) there are mothers. You always appeal to the mums.

TANKY: They should be home burning their kids' toys.

DINGO: No no, look at them. The war is over and we're all going home and you'll be left under a cross, so have a good look ... Now then, how did he (*points to the NCO*) do more than his duty, eh? Look, see here, Tanky, if it was killing, murder, if an officer or NCO does murder when he suggests you do things, when he enthuses you with the wish to please him, for the good reasons he always has ... if that, then would any magistrate in the land take any notice whatsoever of a gallant war record? Eh? What do you hear them all say, eh? Because of your gallant war record or because of your fine military background, eh? Now, they wouldn't say that if it was murder, would they?

TANKY: He killed me.

DINGO: No, look, if he killed you ... if every bloke as went for a shit with a rug wrapped round him blamed it on the bloke who sent him ... see my reasoning?

TANKY: He did.

DINGO: That would make all these public figures who directed the course of events ... well, I hesitate to say it! Every general, colonel, corporal will tell you they hated doing it ...

TANKY: Shouldn't have joined, then. They all lapped it up ... It is very interesting, be fair. He killed me ... and *they* saw it!

DINGO: I can't convince him. He doesn't want to be a hero.

In *The Charge of the Light Brigade* (1968), the film I wrote for Tony Richardson, the character called Lord Raglan comments as he watches Nolan ride off superbly: 'It will be a sad day for England when her soldiers know too well what they are doing. Smacks of murder!'

In *How I Won The War* (1967), a film I wrote at least seven times for Richard Lester before we got it right, Musketeer Gripweed is mortared.

> (*Gripweed stands up suddenly and grins. He then sits down in a field of poppies and watches his blood pool out underneath him, holding his stomach.*)

GRIPWEED: I knew this would happen ... You knew this would happen, didn't you?

> (MUSKETEER CLAPPER *is up against a wall with roses on it. He is grinning and holding off a bayonet with his hands. Mock serious, he says:*)

CLAPPER: Hey, hey — now then.

> (*The bayonet flicks around him, stabbing at him, as the* GERMAN *tries to find a place for it to go in.*)

Here, here — have a heart, eh?

> (*He dies up against the wall, suddenly knowing that it is serious.*)

GRIPWEED: Fought for three reasons — I can't remember what they were. The first reason gets you in ... The reason when you're in is staying alive. I won't know the reason we find afterwards — but it will be a very good one, why it is fought. I'm sure we'll be glad ... and I'm not a thief, really. I've never found anything worth keeping ...

There are those who feel that the Falklands War was inevitable and right, that the operations were carried out with great courage and expertise by the leaders and soldiers of Britain, that it was an expression of British determination to stand up to aggression no matter what the cost in men and matériel and, indeed, that it was a glorious chapter in our history.

There are others who feel the Falklands War should never have happened, and that it *did* happen is a reason for shame, regret and anger.

To go back to Peter Nichols: 'I'm sure you mean to say something of this sort, except that your love of soldiering and the (for me) uninteresting minutiae of military life confuse the issue for someone like me who wants to hear that war's a rotten game but helps maintain the status quo.'

Robert Lawrence and I hold different political views, but we have come together over *Tumbledown* without losing those views. We each believe that our object is achieved. I wrote *Tumbledown* after listening to him, at first uneasily fascinated. It was as if I was being given the chance to talk to a surviving Nolan after his forlorn and frantic ride across the front of the advancing Light Brigade, the opportunity to be around at the beginning of a myth. Lowell Thomas must have licked his lips in much the same way when he set about inventing Lawrence of Arabia. A few thousand years from now, when all myths coalesce, there may come into being a great tragic poem that sings of young men voyaging to icy southern seas to hack and maim and kill with fire and blast and bayonet at the command of a primitive tribal queen demanding restitution of her lovers to her embrace — always supposing we still exist on this earth as singers, that we haven't all been hacked, bombed, blown away by young men fed on myths.

I'm not the poet for such a song, nor is the hero of *Tumbledown* another such as T.E. or Achilles, but another Homer might arise or, from the sangars, another Robert Graves, and at least my Lawrence doesn't start out as a lie. We sat together and I watched him, listened to him, understood him, believed him, became a friend and found his courage, in telling all, heroic.

As for my own feelings about the Falklands War, I feel intense guilt, for I hold it to be wrong that young men like Robert Lawrence were maimed and killed because our skills in avoiding war are not nearly so good as our skills in promoting it.

Charles Wood
March 1987

Tumbledown

Characters

ROBERT LAWRENCE

JOHN LAWRENCE

JEAN LAWRENCE

CHRISTOPHER LAWRENCE

NICK LAWRENCE

HUGH MACKESSAC

HELICOPTER PILOT

CREWMAN

HELEN STUBBS

GEORGE STUBBS

YEOMAN WARDER

DRILL SERGEANT TERRY
KNAPP

SOPHIE

DRUMMER

ADJUTANT

THE 'NOBLE LORD'

PETER FYSHE

LIEUTENANT-COLONEL BILL
KIRKE

ASSISTANT ADJUTANT

SERGEANT WOXEN

TUG

MANDY

CAROL

HENRIETTA

OFFICERS OF THE ROYAL
MARINES

PIPER

PETER WALSH

PAUL GREGORY

STEWART INGLIS

ANGUS TOLLY

MEDICAL OFFICER

HARRY HEBERS

SURGEON (*Fitzroy*)

ASSISTANTS

ORDERLIES

PRISONER

NURSES (*Uganda*)

COLONEL

DOCTOR (*Herald*)

PARA TOM

NURSE (*Herald*)

LEADING RATING

WIRELESS OPERATOR

STEWARD/NURSE (VC10)

RAF OFFICER (Brize Norton)

FAMILIES MAN

FAMILIES WOMAN

NURSES (Brize Norton)

MAN IN WHEELCHAIR

COLOUR SERGEANTS

MALE NURSE (RAF)

NURSES (RAF)

OFFICERS (Princess Mary's
Royal Air Force Nursing
Service)

AIR COMMODORE

DOCTORS (Royal Army Medical
Corps – military hospital)

CAPTAIN (Royal Army Medical
Corps)

LIEUTENANT-COLONEL (Royal Army Medical Corps)
NURSE (military hospital)
PATIENT (neurological hospital)
MARY
NIGHT NURSE 1
NIGHT NURSE 2
YOUNG DOCTOR
OFFICER CADETS (Royal Military Academy, Sandhurst)
SERGEANT (Royal Military Academy, Sandhurst)
HOSPITAL CHAPLAIN
TRICIA
ANGIE
COMPANY SERGEANT-MAJOR BROWN
MAJOR NEWMAN (Queen Alexandra's Royal Army Nursing Corps)
MRS PROTHERO
CABBY
BENNY CODRINGTON
INGRID
TV COMMENTATOR
WHEELCHAIR WOUNDED
LIEUTENANT-COLONEL TAUNTON
DR JESSOPS
OLD MAN (rehabilitation unit)
SERGEANT MARK SMITH
GROUP CAPTAIN (rehabilitation unit)
SQUADRON LEADER WENTWORTH
SALLY
BOB
MAJOR KNOX

MEN MUGGERS
GIRL MUGGER
ARGENTINIAN SOLDIERS (5th Battalion, Naval Infantry Corps)

SCOTS GUARDS
GRENADIER GUARDS
BAND
RATINGS
PILOTS

3 Platoon, Right Flank Co., 2nd Battalion, Scots Guards

SERGEANT BRODICK
LANCE-SERGEANT MCDONALL
CORPORAL BARNES
CORPORAL BAYNES
GUARDSMAN FRASER
GUARDSMAN HORN
GUARDSMEN MUDGE (brothers)
GUARDSMAN O'ROURKE
GUARDSMAN PROTHERO
GUARDSMAN RICHARDS
GUARDSMAN SALTEMARSH
GUARDSMAN WATERSON

Tumbledown

Ext. Day. Through the Cotswolds, England, 1985

Titles over a blue sky and down to the long, winding road high over the Cotswolds near Stow. A green Panther sports car is seen in the distance, approaching along the high, winding road.

Ext. Day. Close on the car

In the car, being driven from London, two young men can be seen behind the windscreen. They talk and laugh. They are obviously friends on good and intimate terms. ROBERT LAWRENCE *is driving.* HUGH MACKESSAC *sits beside him. Both are twenty-three. They listen to loud music. It mingles with the music of the drive whenever the countryside gives us an opportunity to see them close to.*

Ext. Day. Road from the high ground

A twisting descent towards the village is seen from the high road, through a tunnel of trees, dazzlingly green. They drive along a stone-walled lane, farm buildings, a church and into the village, which is low, stone and thatched. They leave the village and pass a farmhouse in an orchard, apple trees, a tyre swung from a low branch. Hanging from an upstairs window is a bedraggled, dirty and long-neglected Union flag.

Ext. Day. Hill out of the village

Sheep are grazing on the hill. The car is being driven out of the small village and up over the crest of a hill; down a curving open road and into a copse of old trees; out of the trees and towards the church at Chastleton; then on and up again to top another rise and see the whole of a county, hills and valleys, undulating gentleness and slow-moving, grazing sheep. A swooping F111 on the way back to Upper Heyford, low-flying, glued to the contours, is followed some few seconds later by another, wagging its wings into a long valley.

Ext. Day. Sports car

R O B E R T'S *fingers, on the joystick of his stereo near the steering wheel, punch up yet another track.*

Ext. Day. Larger village

The car approaching the village along a road lined with thorn. It passes a crumbling tithe barn. There is a deserted stretch of tarmac, then a concrete road, then gates to be opened by H U G H. *A cluster of aerials, complex, beautiful, elegant shapes; on the top of the aerials lights shine red.*

Ext. Day. Georgian house

In the centre of the village, behind gates, high walls, iron railings, is a three-storey house with a portico and a covering of rampant wistaria. The side gates to the courtyard are open, waiting. R O B E R T *drives the Panther through and across the gravel.*

Int. Day. Kitchen of the Stubbses' Georgian house

Stone-flagged floor, dog and cat bowls, an Aga, a dresser filled with pink-and-white crockery, a small dog, two cats, two ducks. H E L E N S T U B B S *looks up apprehensively as she hears the crunch of the gravel and the music, loud, before it is switched off.*

Ext. Day. Sports car

H U G H *gets out. The car is parked over towards the stables. Shots of a granary, a barn, a coach-house.* R O B E R T *gets out, then leans into the car for his cigarettes. Finding them, looks up at the house.*

Surprise cut to:
Ext. Dawn. Prow of a ship at sea

An empty, shimmering sea. In the prow of a ship facing the direction of movement is R O B E R T L A W R E N C E. *Wind, spray.*

Ext. Day. Courtyard

R O B E R T, *walking towards the house, gives another glance upwards, this time at the sky.*

Main Title: *Tumbledown*

Ext. Day. Mt Tumbledown, Falkland Islands, 14 June 1982

Sky. The sound of a helicopter. Flurries of snow. The sound of wind in the crags is like tentative pipe music punctuated by quite unreal slugs of silence, so that later, when men shout, their mouths can be seen to open but no sound comes forth. The edge of a Scout helicopter, a black wedge, intrudes for a moment into the defined patch of sky and moves out again. Its rotors disturb the air and the snow particles, producing distinct patterns, though the helicopter is not seen.

End of Main Titles

Int. Day. Kitchen of Stubbs House

HELEN STUBBS, *her husband* GEORGE, HUGH *and* ROBERT *are eating lunch: shepherd's pie, a big bottle of red wine, bread, fruit, cheese.*

Ext. Day. Mt Tumbledown

Sky. Faces looking down. Mouths opening. The noise of the helicopter, in and out, and the noise of the wind. Faces of men of the Scots Guards, bloody, dirty, cold, eyes sharp with an excitement not yet dulled. The helicopter lifting to show on its turn the sea, crags, the unmistakable shape of the Falkland Islands, before dropping and settling for a low flight.

Int. Day. Scout helicopter

The PILOT *turns away from Tumbledown Mountain. Both casualty-evacuation 'coffins' on his skids have their occupants. They are not recognizable because of blood, mud and matted hair, but one of them is* ROBERT LAWRENCE. *The fuel gauge of the helicopter registers empty, just. The* CREWMAN *points with gloved finger. The* PILOT *nods philosophically as he drops over water, then he points with his own gloved hand down at the surface of the sea.*
PILOT: Look, a seal . . .

Ext. Day. Shimmering sea below

A seal swims with the shadow of the helicopter on the surface for a brief moment before the helicopter turns away across land, a fast, low, hopeful run. Music.

7

Int. Day. Kitchen of Stubbs house

The small dog of the house is sniffing gently at ROBERT'*s left hand.* ROBERT *is finishing his food.*

ROBERT: I was conscious all the time. I never ever lost consciousness.

HUGH: You were bloody lucky.

ROBERT: Yes.

HUGH: No, I mean the pilot disobeyed orders when he heard we had wounded. He'd been in the Scots Guards, a colour sergeant. Got the DFC.

ROBERT: The Scout was very vulnerable, I'm sure we lost a lot of Scout helicopters to small-arms fire.

HUGH: You were extremely lucky.

HELEN: Would you like some more shepherd's pie?

HUGH: I'd love some. Starving. Way he drives terrifies me.

ROBERT: That's another story, driving.

GEORGE: It's a marvellous car, Robert. What is it?

ROBERT: Panther.

HUGH: It isn't a car — it's a statement.

ROBERT: It is really. Damn good car as well.

HUGH: I wouldn't mind if you didn't smack me in the chops with your left arm every time you're forced to brake.

ROBERT: It's called clonus. It only happens when I'm scared . . . (*Grins.*) You have to be ready to duck.

Ext. Night. Traitor's Gate, Tower of London

Floodlights. SPECTATORS *watching the Ceremony of the Keys. Tower of London Guard, provided by the Second Battalion of the Scots Guards (2 SG) formed up. Lieutenant* ROBERT LAWRENCE *has marched to their front and halted. Footsteps are heard approaching. Anticipation. Then a stamp of feet and a scream of rage causes some* SPECTATORS *to flinch, others to duck, others to giggle with fright, as a hitherto unremarkable sentry, pacing majestically and soothingly to the rear, throws his rifle into the on-guard position and, in broad, placeless Scots, challenges the Escort to the Keys.*

PROTHERO: Ahlt! Wha gaes thair?

YEOMAN WARDER: The keys!

PROTHERO: Whaaaaase kays?

(Just on the edge of the floodlights SGT BRODICK *and two* GUARDSMEN

who form the Escort to the Keys with a YEOMAN WARDER *stand halted by the challenge.*)

YEOMAN WARDER: Queen Elizabeth the Second's Keys!

(ROBERT, *to his rear a* DRUMMER, *brings the Tower of London Guard up to attention.*)

ROBERT: Tower of London Guard, 'SHUN! Tower of London Guard, shoulder ARMS!

(*Escort to the Keys full in the floodlights now and halted as* ROBERT *gives the order.*)

Tower of London Guard, present ARMS!

(MRS JOHN LAWRENCE *and* JOHN LAWRENCE *watch their son from among the spectators. They are in their middle fifties, he a retired wing commander who sports an RAF moustache but not stuffy. With them, standing near,* DRILL SERGEANT TERRY KNAPP *in his thirties, known to them, six feet six inches tall and very smart. They are joined by* SOPHIA MARTIN-WELLS, *a young girl, attractive, well-dressed.* ROBERT *has drawn his sword in salute. The* DRUMMER *sounds the Last Post.* ROBERT *stands stock-still, affected by the sound. Faint noise of drums, not the usual military ones.*)

Surprise cut to:
Ext. Dawn. Prow of the ship at sea

ROBERT *is in the prow. The drums sound harsh, clear, metallic and warning. The first snatches of a song are heard: 'I will go, I will go/When the fighting is over/To the land of . . .*

Ext. Night. Traitor's Gate, Tower of London

The last notes of the bugle. The YEOMAN WARDER *doffs his hat.*

YEOMAN WARDER: (*Loud and clear*) God Bless Queen Elizabeth the Second!

(*As one man, the Tower of London Guard respond.*)

GUARD: Amen!

Ext. Night. Southampton

Troops in combat dress are embarking on the Canberra. *Floodlights. A band is playing. Flags, banners, cheers, singing.*

Int. Night. Guardroom corridor, Tower of London

GUARDSMEN (*Scots Guards*), *in Home Service Dress, clattering off parade in the tight corridor — rifles, bearskins, racks, click of boots on stone, a whistle, television.*

Int. Night. Officer's flat, Tower of London

ROBERT *takes off his tunic to expose a white T-shirt with a pop-group blazon of pink and orange and the electric legend 'Human League' under the braces holding up his tweeds. His blue patrols have been laid out ready for him on the bed by his orderly,* LUMPY (GDSM HORN), *who is twenty and wears a smart brown suit, white shirt and sharp, narrow tie. Next door the television set is on for* The Nine O'Clock News. JOHN LAWRENCE *has a glass of scotch,* JEAN LAWRENCE *a gin and tonic,* TERRY KNAPP *a glass of beer.*

TERRY KNAPP: Cheers, Mr Lawrence, sorr.

JOHN: Cheers, Drill Sergeant.

ROBERT: Was Sophie there, daddy?

JEAN: She thought she wouldn't come up.

JOHN: Yes, she was, Spud.

> (*On the television screen the men of 3 Para and 40, 42, 45 Royal Marine Commandos line the rails of the* Canberra *as it leaves Southampton for the South Atlantic.* ROBERT LAWRENCE, *who has come out to join the others, watches.*)

ROBERT: (*Dutifully but incuriously*) What was it like tonight, Drill Sergeant?

TERRY KNAPP: No' bad, sorr.

ROBERT: When it's bad, it's very, very bad. When it's no' bad, it's brilliant . . .

JEAN: I know it's coming, but when the sentry challenges in broad Scots, 'Halt-who-goes-there?', I always . . .

ROBERT: That was Prothero tonight . . .

JEAN: . . . jump out of my skin.

ROBERT: He's not a Scot. He just puts the voice on for Public Duties.

> (ROBERT *glares at the screen, rubbing his forehead where the red mark made by his bearskin is still vivid. Suddenly he erupts in anger and frustration, flinging himself into a chair.*)

Look at them! Paras! Look at them! Marines! The whole world could go to war and we would be as likely to go as walk on the moon. Public duties!

TERRY KNAPP: They'll be back. They'll no' finish it. Tickets. Twice round the islands and away home is what will occur, sorr.

ROBERT: Bloody Paras . . . Look at that one, his beret over his eyes. A real Tom that one, the maroon machine.

TERRY KNAPP: Aye, well, be all over when they get down there, sorr, and very, very cold.

Surprise cut to
Ext. Night. Tumbledown diversion

TERRY KNAPP *is in beret and combat dress. His face is camouflaged, alert, strong, but looking suddenly perplexed.*

Int. Day. Kitchen of Stubbs house

ROBERT *lifts his left hand and arm up on to the table to put his hand at the side of the plate. He feels in his left-hand pocket for the cigarettes he keeps there.*

ROBERT: I know you don't like smoking – Hugh has told me. But would you mind?

HELEN: No, please.

ROBERT: The first to be killed . . . one of them. I wasn't there. It was before us. . .

HUGH: Got him straight between the eyes. Drill Sergeant, do you see? So well balanced on his feet that he didn't fall. Braced, they tell me. Nobody knew he'd been hit.

ROBERT: That's crap.

HUGH: That's what I was told.

ROBERT: You fall, Hugh. I did.

HUGH: That's what I was told . . .

(ROBERT *gets to his feet with an apologetic smile.*)

ROBERT: When I have to go, I have to go awfully fast. That's another thing . . .

GEORGE: Yes, of course. Let me show you.

(HELEN *watches them go.*)

HELEN: It wasn't until he lifted his left hand up on to the table that I really thought about him being paralysed.

HUGH: Oh, yes, he is – the whole of his left side, basically. I swore he was dead when I saw him.

11

Ext. Day. Street near Chelsea Barracks

PROTHERO *comes out of the squat he lives in opposite the barracks — a skinhead, all the gear. Anything less like a guardsman is hard to imagine.* ROBERT *is hurrying along the street, in a leather jacket and trilby, towards the barracks. He is equipped with a Sony Walkman. Anything less like a guards officer is hard to imagine.*

ROBERT: Pongo!

PROTHERO: Och, awa, sir — left me Walkman, haven't I?
(PROTHERO *puts his heels together for a brief moment and then dashes back in for his own Sony Walkman.*)

Ext. Day. Chelsea Barracks

HUGH *and* ROBERT *hurry, slightly late, across the parade ground to where the* ADJUTANT *is about to inspect subaltern officers in their Home Service Dress. Several of them are there, among them a very young officer, just joined, called* PETER FYSHE, *and a scion of the aristocracy called 'the* NOBLE LORD'. ROBERT *is inspected, then* HUGH, *who has a tunic-collar hook undone.*

ADJUTANT: Mr Mackessac, did anyone check your dress?

HUGH: Of course, sir. Mr Lawrence.

ADJUTANT: Next time, Mr Lawrence, do it properly.

ROBERT: You . . . Mackessac!

Int. Day. Officers' Mess, Chelsea Barracks

ROBERT *is on the telephone.* HUGH *and* PETER FYSHE *are talking and drinking coffee.*

HUGH: Bobbit is leaving us.

PETER: Really?

HUGH: 14 Intelligence Company want him.

PETER: What do they do?

HUGH: Not allowed to know, Peter, not allowed to know, but it will be under the turf in Armagh, I should think, or under a dirty mackintosh . . .

PETER: Oh? Why would he want to?

HUGH: He wants to do everything. Jungle warfare . . . he's done it all. He is, despite appearances, a real action man is Bobbit. Do they want you?
(ROBERT *comes back from the telephone.*)

ROBERT: They wouldn't want you.

HUGH: I wouldn't want them. Far too dangerous.

Ext. Day. Street near Chelsea Barracks

ROBERT *out running with his platoon, 3 Platoon Right Flank Co., 2 SG, all in track suits. Among them* PROTHERO, LUMPY, SALTEMARSH, O'ROURKE, WATERSON, SGT MCDONALL, CPL BAYNES.

Int. Day. Kitchen of Stubbs house

GEORGE *comes back from showing* ROBERT *to the lavatory through a passage with military prints on the walls — huge, Victorian bravery.* HUGH *lights a cigarette.*

HUGH: Did Louise say anything?

HELEN: Haven't you spoken to her?

HUGH: She knew we were going to call in on the way to Shropshire.

HELEN: Yes, but she did say she might not be here in time.

HUGH: She isn't. (*He laughs once, a short, nervous, rueful bark. His hands tremble. He bites his nails.*)

GEORGE: I do find Robert fascinating. I find it all fascinating. You've never talked much about it, Hugh.

HUGH: Oh, I have, George. Do nothing else. (*Pause.*) Perhaps not.

Ext. Day. Mt Tumbledown

A gush of blood all over SGT MCDONALL *when he takes off* ROBERT's *beret.* CPL BAYNES *has dragged* ROBERT *from where he fell on to a slab of rock near the top of the crags of Tumbledown. The blood has gushed in one released splash all over the front of* MCDONALL, *his arms, his face.* ROBERT *has watched it happen. There is sniper fire, which is returned, and the crump of artillery from Stanley.* ROBERT *is laid down, face up to the sky.*

HUGH: Has anyone thought of packing snow round it?

> (HUGH *stands over* ROBERT, *looking down at him, an Argentinian FN rifle in each hand. He looks at the wound in* ROBERT's *head. A shell lands near. It doesn't go off. It's a dud.*)

(*Yells*) Get away from him!

> (ROBERT *is left stretched on the slab of rock. Seen from above he is alone, looking up at the sky. He is obviously in great pain and rubbing his head and protruding brain into the mud in an effort to relieve the pain. He is talking; when close, one can hear him saying over and over again:*)

ROBERT: The buggers think I'm dead. The buggers think I'm dead. The buggers think I'm dead ...

> (*Snow flurries across him. More single shots from the sniper's rifle.*)

13

Ext. Day. Street near Chelsea Barracks

The platoon runs in time in track suits and boots. ROBERT *is with them, very fit, grinning, singing, sweat on his forehead.* PROTHERO, *running near, looks like a real skinhead. All the platoon are into the rhythm as they approach the barracks and go through the gates.* ROBERT *leading, they chant.*

PLATOON: Ain't no sense in looking down.
        Ain't no sense in looking down.
        Ain't no discharge on the ground.
        Ain't no discharge on the ground.
        Am I right or wrong?
        You're RIGHT!
        Am I going strong?
        You're RIGHT!
        Sound off!
        One, two . . .
        Sound off!
        Three, four . . .
        Bring it on down!
        One, two, three, four.
        ONE-TWO! THREE-FOUR!

Intercut with:
Int./Ext. Day. Officers' Mess, Chelsea Barracks

A window, seen from outside and inside. LT COL BILL KIRKE, *the Commanding Officer of 2 SG, with the* ASSISTANT ADJUTANT. HUGH *is passing as the strains lift upwards.*

HUGH: (*Laughing nervously*) Not quite Brigade of Guards, sir.
BILL KIRKE: No. But it's all right. What's your platoon doing, Hugh?
PLATOON: . . . in lookin' good.
        Ought to be in Hollywood.
        Ought to be in Hollywood.
        Am I right or wrong?
        You're RIGHT!
        Am I going strong?
        You're RIGHT!
HUGH: Boots, sir. I thought boots. The major-general is very hot on boots this year, I am told by a Grenadier of his acquaintance.

Int. Day. Kitchen of Stubbs house

The sound of the water rushing into the tank as the flush of the lavatory is pulled and then ROBERT LAWRENCE *comes back into the kitchen.*

ROBERT: You see, I hate cripples. Always have done. And I will not be one. That's what they don't seem to understand – I will not be a cripple. It isn't just my leg, my hand. Sometimes I don't get there in time . . . my arm. Did this time, though, you'll be glad to know . . .

HUGH: Show them the photographs, Bobbit.

ROBERT: Do you think I ought?

HUGH: You always do.

ROBERT: I don't think I should. I don't think Helen should see them. I mean, people faint. We made this pact, Hugh and I, that he would shoot me, I'd shoot him, if anything ghastly happened. Maimed or anything.

GEORGE: Why didn't you?

HUGH: Too many people around, I suppose. And anyway he spoke to me.

ROBERT: What did I say?

HUGH: You always ask me that. Some rubbish about being cold. We were all bloody cold.

ROBERT: I think I was very near colder than most.

HUGH: Yes, you've said that before too.

ROBERT: Come on, Hugh, what did I say?

HUGH: You said, 'Tell Sophie I love her.' I don't remember it, but that's what you say you said.

Ext. Day. Mt Tumbledown

Robert is being cuddled by SGT WOXEN, *a battalion piper and medic. He is shivering and shouting. Shots can be heard. Then a shout from* SGT BRODICK.

ROBERT: Where are the sleeping-bag liners? Every platoon should carry two extra, for the cold, for the casualties, for me. Where's the helicopter? Can't use morphine – it's a head wound. Can't get a helicopter up here. Too close. No casevac. Too close. Where's the helicopter?

(*Faces, close, dirty, excited. An* ARGENTINIAN SOLDIER *of the 5th Naval Infantry is pushed over* ROBERT *by men of his platoon or perhaps by other men. The whole scene is very odd and unreal. The voices of the*

n become a crazy jumble of hoarse shouts; the ARGENTINIAN SOL-
IER, *pushed down, is grinning or wincing in pain. Nothing is certain
or clear. The Scots accents of the men become thicker in their excitement,
jubilation, anger.)*

VOICES: This is the one did for Mr Lawrence ... This bugger killed
him. He's no' dead. He's no' dead, do you see, Fernando? You didnae
kill him, Fernando ... The sauce of him. The spic bastard, he sur-
rendered ... *Rindanse*, Fernando! *Manos arriba!*

(*Then light, sky. The faces are gone.* ROBERT *hears one shot, then more
shots.*)

Int. Night. Tug and Mandy's

*Frank Sinatra sings. Low lighting. A small bar and restaurant on the Fulham
Road.* ROBERT *is behind the bar in bomber jacket and jeans.* HUGH *is at a
table with two girls,* CAROL *and* HENRIETTA. *He has come in with two other*
GUARDS OFFICERS *in more conventional civilian clothes than* ROBERT'S.
TUG *is the owner and barman. His wife is* MANDY. *He is Hungarian, late
thirties. She is the same age, Cockney, attractive. Both are very fond of*
ROBERT *and allow him behind the cocktail bar.*

TUG: Ought you not to be sleeping, Robert?

ROBERT: Piss off, Tug. Going to the Falklands, Tug.

TUG: I know ... But it is very late for you, Robert. For you if you are
going early. For you, Robert.

ROBERT: What about Hugh?

TUG: I don't care about Hugh. It is you. We don't care about Hugh, do
we, Mandy?

MANDY: There're soldiers down the other end, Robert, talking about it.
Are they Guards?

ROBERT: No. Why don't you care about Hugh?

TUG: You come to us long before Hugh.

ROBERT: I do ... I did. Oh, I am drunk, Tug. I really am drunk, to be
honest. Basically pissed ... Marines. They're Marines. I hate Marines.

TUG: I know, but don't fight, eh?

HUGH: How wide is that door, Tug?

TUG: Wide?

HUGH: Is it wide enough for a wheelchair?

TUG: I don't know. How wide is a wheelchair?

MANDY: Oh, don't be morbid ...

16

ROBERT: It is essential that we know, Tug. My friend Hugh must know. And the stairs — will we get it down the stairs?

HUGH: Have you got a tape measure, Tug? How wide are wheelchairs?

ROBERT: Basically they're . . . that wide. A bum's width. Because of their purpose, basically. I hate Paras as well.

(ROBERT *glares at two* OFFICERS *of the Royal Marines in civvies as he goes to measure the door.*)

Get a tape measure, Tug. We need specifications.

(HUGH *is on the stairs already. He shakes his head doubtfully, measuring with his arms.* CAROL *and* HENRIETTA *come to the bottom of the stairs with* ROBERT, *who surveys the stairs.*)

Where is Sophie? Carol? Henrietta? Where is she?

HUGH: Never do it. Tug, this may be the last time Robert ever visits this establishment on the Fulham Road . . .

(TUG *gives a tape measure to* CAROL, *shrugging and laughing but beginning to dislike the game being played. He shakes his head at* MANDY, *who voices her disapproval.*)

MANDY: Stop them, Tug. I don't like it.

ROBERT: If . . . When . . . Will you shoot me, Hugh, basically? You are my friend. I ask you . . .

HUGH: Will you do the same for me?

ROBERT: Shut up. Listen . . . Of course. Listen, I'm talking about me. When I'm maimed, mutilated, my dick shot off, whatever, you must promise to finish me off.

HUGH: Yes.

ROBERT: Promise.

TUG: This is going too far . . .

(ROBERT, *deadly serious now and very strong, clutches* HUGH *tightly by his coat.* ROBERT *pushes him down the stairs, slapping his cheek with his other hand.*)

ROBERT: Promise! Promise!

HUGH: My dear Bobbit . . .

(HUGH *tries to remove his hands, but* ROBERT *is much stronger.* HUGH *goes cold.*)

Just shut it, will you? Just calm down.

ROBERT: Promise.

HUGH: All right, I promise. Damn it, there is nothing I would like better than to blow your bloody brains out!

TUG: Get out. I've had enough. Out of here, please. Please!

ROBERT: That's all I want to know . . .

> (ROBERT *walks a little unsteadily back to the bar, glaring at the* MARINES, *who would rather not have any trouble, grinning at them suddenly as he sits at the bar.* HUGH *is being bustled out by* TUG.)

HUGH: All right, I'm going, Tug.

MANDY: Where's Sophie then, Robert?

ROBERT: Haven't seen her in weeks.

TUG: That man is not your friend, Robert . . .

> (SOPHIE *has arrived, behind* ROBERT. MANDY *has seen her and waves, pointing at* ROBERT.)

ROBERT: Yes, he is, Tug. He'll do it. To be honest, he'll do what I tell him.

TUG: That's enough!

SOPHIE: Hello, Robert.

ROBERT: Hello. They've gone — Carol and Henrietta, and Hugh, all the crowd . . .

SOPHIE: I know. I saw them. Robert, I'm sorry about the last few weeks.

ROBERT: Been hectic, have they?

SOPHIE: Sort of.

ROBERT: Yes, that's it . . . sort of.

SOPHIE: Knew you'd be here.

ROBERT: Good. Last night, you know. Last night.

Ext. Night. Chelsea pub

A PIPER *squeezes his pipes just once. The pub is full of* GUARDSMEN; *the* PIPER *is outside.*

Ext. Day. The prow of the ship

ROBERT *is in the prow. There is a metallic, warning rattle of drums.*

Ext. Night. Chelsea pub

The full sound of the bagpipes and PROTHERO *catapults from the pub, followed by* SALTEMARSH, O'ROURKE *and other members of 3 Platoon Right Flank Co., 2 SG, the* BROTHERS MUDGE, RICHARDS *and others, all of the Scots Guards, all in civvies, all following the* PIPER *back to the barracks.*

PROTHERO *dances ahead with his arms in the air, football days. A* YOUNG
GUARDSMAN, *not of 3 Platoon, runs behind him.*

YOUNG GUARDSMAN: Pongo!

PROTHERO: Don't call me Pongo! Do you hear?

> (*His knuckles display the word H.A.T.E. The* YOUNG GUARDSMAN *is
> rapped down by* PROTHERO. O'ROURKE *runs up to be with* PROTH-
> ERO. SALTEMARSH, WATERSON *and* LUMPY *hug him, then raise their
> arms up and prance, football days. They march, the* PIPER *playing for all
> he is worth.*)

O'ROURKE: Why did the chicken cross the road?

PROTHERO: Sound off!

OTHERS: One, two!

PROTHERO: Sound off!

OTHERS: Three, four!

PROTHERO: Bring it on down!

ALL: One, two, three, four! ONE-TWO! THREE-FOUR!

Ext. Night. Chelsea Barracks

*The metallic beat of drums is heard over the scene of apparent chaos and
departure. Coaches in the barracks are being loaded by* PROTHERO *and the
others.* SGT BRODICK *is there.* TERRY KNAPP *towers amiably over everyone.
All are in combat dress; all have their weapons. The coaches, hired from civilian
firms, give the proceedings a strange, supporters' club triviality. A group of
senior officers looks on: the commanding officer,* BILL KIRKE; *his* ADJUTANT;
his company commanders, PETER WALSH (*Right Flank*), PAUL GREGORY
(*Left Flank*); STEWART INGLIS, *blond, very Action Man; the padre,* ANGUS
TOLLY; *the* MEDICAL OFFICER. *Suitcases are going into the coaches,
together with kit bags.* HUGH MACKESSAC, *in combat dress, the worse for
wear, is looking for* ROBERT.

HUGH: Sergeant Brodick, have you see Mr Lawrence?

BRODICK (*Loyally*): He's around, sir.

HUGH: Quite. Where?

> (*The* NOBLE LORD *is looking slightly confused, with his platoon sergeant.*
> HUGH *is seen to ask him. Then* LUMPY *is seen carrying two rifles.*)

Mr Lawrence?

LUMPY: Sir?

HUGH: That his rifle?

LUMPY: Sir.

19

HUGH: Sergeant Brodick, this is serious, have you actually seen Mr Lawrence?

BRODICK: No, sir. I have not.

HUGH: Damn! Who has a car?

(HUGH *hurries off towards a group of* GRENADIER OFFICERS *who are gathered to see the* SCOTS GUARDS *leave, champagne bottles in their hands. Some* SCOTS GUARDS OFFICERS *are with them.* HUGH *pulls* HARRY HEBERS *out of the group.*)

HARRY: Hugh, have some champagne.

(*He pushes a bottle down* HUGH's *combat jacket front.*)

HUGH: (*Quietly but urgently*) Harry, Robert hasn't turned up.

HARRY: Where is he?

HUGH: I don't bloody know. There's his orderly wandering about with two rifles ... Home, I suppose.

HARRY: Come on!

(HUGH *and* HARRY *leave the barracks.* HUGH *is called back by the* GUARD COMMANDER *and his rifle is taken from him.*)

Ext. Night. Chelsea street

HARRY *is driving.* HUGH *is with him in* HARRY's *little Spitfire, which is going very fast through the empty street.*

Int. Night. Robert's flat

ROBERT *is asleep with* SOPHIE. *The sound of the car drawing up outside. The headlights are seen in the basement flat. Then* HARRY *and* HUGH *run down the steps. They bang on the door.* ROBERT *doesn't hear them.* SOPHIE *does. She sits up and tries to waken* ROBERT, *who is dead to the world.* HUGH *and* HARRY *break down the door.* ROBERT *is pulled from the bed.*

HUGH: Robert, come on!

HARRY: Hello.

ROBERT: Oh, God, what time is it?

HARRY: Come on. Get your clothes on. Come on, just get them together. Get your trousers on.

ROBERT: Crumbs, what time is it?

(ROBERT *grabs his clothes and pulls them on — combat dress, pullover, beret. Half dressed, he is dragged out by* HUGH.)

HUGH: We'll take your car, Harry.

ROBERT: Here, my keys ...

(He tosses his car keys to HARRY, *who is helping him to dress.* SOPHIE *is trying to find her clothes in a jumble of bedclothes,* ROBERT's *clothes, her own.* ROBERT *and* HUGH *go.* ROBERT *comes back for his Sony Walkman. There is a shout from* HUGH *outside.* ROBERT *hurriedly kisses* SOPHIE *and goes. She pulls on his T-shirt, marked 'Human League'.* HARRY *and* SOPHIE, *formal, polite, innocent, shake hands.)*

HARRY: Hello. We haven't met. I'm Harry Hebers. Grenadier Guards.
SOPHIE: I'm Sophia Martin-Wells. Hello.

Int. Night. Coach

ROBERT *is in the coach, his beret pulled down over his forehead. Hunched, he is sitting on his own, his Sony Walkman on. Around him is his platoon, all silent. There is just the tinny noise of the Walkmans. Light shines on their faces from sodium street lighting outside as they go through a town.* HUGH *is sitting across the aisle on his own. Both are alone with their thoughts. Everybody is very quiet. The faces of all the platoon look out, none asleep, all sober, as they go through the town's empty streets on the way to Southampton. The drums start.*

Int. Day. Cabin of *Queen Elizabeth the Second*

Outside, the noise of cheering crowds and a band playing. In the small cabin there are bergens (rucksacks), suitcases, rifles, two camp beds on the floor. ROBERT *and* HUGH *stand there. The porthole is open. Now they look shattered. Each pulls a bottle of champagne from his combat jacket.*

ROBERT: No smoking in the cabin.
HUGH: Bloody hell.
ROBERT: Peter Walsh says he won't have it.
HUGH: We'll have to do it in the bog then, won't we?
ROBERT: Sitting in the bog moaning about dying.
HUGH: Sounds like the idea.
ROBERT: At least I saw Sophie.
HUGH: We all saw Sophie.

  *(*PETER WALSH's *equipment is on the only bed. The* NOBLE LORD *puts his head round the door after knocking.)*

NOBLE LORD: Robert, Hugh, platoon commanders in the Perfumery...
  (Grinning, he leaves.)

ROBERT: I suppose Lieutenant the Noble Lord's got a cabin of his own.

HUGH: Probably got the padre.

ROBERT: That's all right. Angus wouldn't stop us smoking.

   (*The drums again.*)

Ext. Dawn. The prow of the ship

ROBERT *is in the prow. The song starts up.*

Ext./ Int. Day and night. QE2 sequence

Action takes place in the following locations: Boat Deck reading room, dance floor of the Double Down Room, spiral staircase, Queen's Room, shopping arcade, band room, card room and Quarter Deck, with its vast information map, as well as exteriors like muster stations.

ROBERT *and his platoon, in T-shirts, combat trousers and boots, pound the decks and the hardboard.*

GPMGS firing out to sea, PROTHERO *with his,* SGT BRODICK *with others.*

Rows of blue and orange civilian bergens are being painted green.

Group photograph: the three platoon commanders, HUGH, ROBERT *and the* NOBLE LORD, *with* SGT BRODICK *and two other platoon sergeants behind each officer.*

Men run in full equipment, with weapons, up and down the stairs and gangways of the ship and through the bizarre shopping arcade ('Cosmetics', 'Perfumery', 'Boutique'), one platoon going one way, another the other. All the time GURKHAS *are wandering around blindfolded. All the* OFFICERS *of 2SG are seen with their men, up and down the spiral staircase.*

There is a map of the Falkland Islands on the huge wall of the Quarter Deck. Maps are spread in the cabins. The INFORMATION OFFICER *is giving information on the enemy. In the Brigade HQ there are more maps, more information, notes.*

ROBERT *is passing on information to his platoon, his note book full of jottings. Rifles are being painted or strips of hessian are being wound round their stocks, first field dressings taped to them.*

Int. Night. Canteen, QE2

ROBERT *is sitting at a table in the very crowded canteen with his platoon. Near him are* LUMPY, SALTEMARSH, O'ROURKE *and* PROTHERO. *The rest are around.*

ROBERT: *Manos arriba* — that's all you need to know. It's Spanish for 'Hands up'.

PROTHERO: *Manos arriba! Manos* bleedin' *arriba*, Jimmy!

ROBERT: Brilliant.

(*Cans of McEwan are on the table. All are drinking the beer.* ROBERT *starts to rattle his can on the table like the beat of the drums in the song. Then he starts to sing and the whole platoon joins in.*)

> I will go, I will go,
> When the fighting is over
> To the land of McCleod
> That I left to be a soldier,
> I will go, I will go . . .

Song over:

Ext. Day. Deck of QE2

Right Flank Co. is doing pokey drill on the flight deck, led by PETER WALSH, *the company commander. Behind them is Left Flank Co., led by* PAUL GREGORY. ROBERT *and* HUGH *are with their platoons.*

Int. Night. Corridor, QE2

ROBERT's *platoon is gathered in the corridor, near the hairdressing boutique.* ROBERT *is giving them instructions on how to get into a landing craft.*

ROBERT: The drill is that you give your bergen and rifle to the man on your right and move under the instruction of the man on left. When you're aboard, you remain quiet and do as you're told. And no smoking. Is that clear?

(*The song is heard over this.*)

Ext. Day. Landing craft

Very wet and very cold. The whole company is aboard. Some men are so cold that they are shivering uncontrollably. SALTEMARSH *is looking particularly bad. The song is heard over this.*

Ext. Dawn. The march to Bluff Cove

Looming out of the early-morning mist are the huge shapes of 3 Platoon, their bergens towering above them. ROBERT *is in the lead,* SGT BRODICK *bringing up the rear.* LUMPY, *with radio, is with* ROBERT. STEWART INGLIS *slithers*

and scrambles past on a motor bike, the picture of the blond-beast fighting man.
He gives a cheery wave to ROBERT *and goes on ahead to get stuck in some*
mud. The platoon trudges past. INGLIS *calls out for help.* PROTHERO *gives*
him the one-finger salute.

PROTHERO: Climb on this, Action Man!

    (ROBERT *is delighted. Though dirty, tired, cold, he is in his element.*)

Ext. Dawn. The prow of the ship

The ship is approaching a low stretch of land shrouded in mist. ROBERT *is still*
in the prow, the wind on his face. The song can still be heard over.

Ext. Day. Bluff Cove

3 Platoon is digging trenches. SALTEMARSH *is shivering in the half-dug*
trench. ROBERT *and* HUGH *are at an O-group in the shearing shed.*

PETER WALSH: The assault on Tumbledown is confirmed. As we
expected, the Battalion will move to map reference 295715, which is
Goat Ridge. Then, when Two Sisters have been taken, we will move
as a battalion from the saddle to Tumbledown Mountain, ref. 325722,
fight along the ridge of the mountain until we stop, then 1/7 Gurkha
Rifles will take over and bat on to take Mt William through us ...

    (SALTEMARSH *collapses in the trench. He lies there, shivering, at the*
    bottom of the trench, which has filled up with six inches of freezing water.
    Around him the rest of the platoon are digging in. He goes into convulsions.
    ROBERT *looks down at him. A moment's hesitation, then he jumps into*
    the trench and drags SALTEMARSH, *who is a very big man, out on to*
    the ground.)

ROBERT: (*Shouts*) Sgt. Brodick!

    (SALTEMARSH *has stopped breathing.* ROBERT *gives him the kiss of*
    life, still shouting for SGT BRODICK *as he does so.* SGT BRODICK *runs*
    towards the trench with PROTHERO *and others.*)

He's breathing again, but he had gone into convulsions. Get him to
the sheds.

    (*They start to half drag, half carry* SALTEMARSH *towards the sheds.*
    ROBERT *feels his pulse.*)

His heart has stopped. Put him down.

    (ROBERT *starts to massage* SALTEMARSH's *heart.* BRODICK *feels the*
    pulse.)

Is it going again? Right ...

(*They drag* SALTEMARSH *again. Rain, flurries of sleet. His breathing stops again; again* ROBERT *gives him the kiss of life. Then* SALTEMARSH *has a choking fit. His breathing stops yet again.*)

SGT BRODICK: I cannot feel his heart. There's nae breathing, sorr ... Let me, sorr.

ROBERT: No, no.

(ROBERT *is angry. He tugs* SALTEMARSH *up by the hair and boots him hard in the back, then drops him in the mud again to check and listen.*)
He's all right. That did it. Now get him in under cover.

(*They are nearer the sheds now.* LUMPY *lumbers up to help, then* SALTEMARSH *goes again, and* ROBERT *once more gives him the kiss of life. This time, when he comes round he vomits.*)
You rotten bastard, Saltemarsh.

Int. Night. The Lawrences' house, Barnes

JEAN LAWRENCE *is going to bed. Their dachshund whimpers at the foot of the bed.*

JEAN: What's the matter with you, you silly dog? What's the matter with you? Nobody is going to hurt you. You're all right. Don't make such a noise.

Ext. Day. Goat Ridge

ROBERT *and his platoon, in light battle order, their bergens left behind, trudge up over a small ridge. There is artillery fire from Argentinian positions and open ground ahead of them with no cover from the shelling. The* ADJUTANT *pokes* ROBERT *in the chest with his walking stick.*

ADJUTANT: You do well, Robert, but take care of yourself.

Surprise cut to
Int. Day. Fitzroy refrigeration plant

ROBERT *is being lifted on to an operating table in the incredible place.* SURGEONS, DOCTORS *and* ORDERLIES *are wearing see-through, disposable plastic aprons and masks. The operating theatre, lights, equipment, tables are set up in the most appalling conditions imaginable.* ROBERT, *with a drip in his arm, is fully conscious still. He is in very great pain but capable of complaining.*

ROBERT: Look here, I've been waiting for four hours. You thought I was going to die. They cut my boots off — was that strictly necessary? I tie my bootlaces in a particular way, so that one cut of the lace and they come off. I told him that, but he cut straight through the leather. They were my Northern Ireland boots. What on earth is the point of tying one's boots . . .? And it's bloody cold waiting out there in the corridor . . .

(*All this nowhere near so coherent to those around him as it is to* ROBERT, *whose voice fluctuates from very low to grumbling, grunting loud but is constant. He is very weak and is having blood. He has lost a great deal of blood. The* SURGEONS *deal with his horrific wound, in spite of his complaints, efficiently and quickly. Photographs are taken of the head wound. There is a flash. The field dressings have been taken off. A phosphorus grenade rolls from his smock on to the floor. All the* SURGEONS *and* ASSISTANTS *step back.* ROBERT *tries to laugh.*)

(*Hisses amiably*) It's all right. You can't get the bloody pins out of them even when you want to. Need a pair of pliers. Everybody should carry a pair of pliers . . .

(ASSISTANTS *cut off the smock while the* SURGEONS *examine the wound.* ROBERT *complains bitterly.*)

The last straw. This is my SAS smock. Let me take it off. I can take it off . . .

(*A Browning pistol is found in the smock.* ROBERT *tries to keep it, his hand reaching for it. It drops from him.*)

I want it. Took that from an Argie. You should see him. If you think I look bad, you should see him . . .

SURGEON: It's all right — Robert, is it? It's all right. You can have it back later. Speak to Barnaby about it. He'll let you have it back.

(*He looks at the pistol before giving it to an* ORDERLY *and examines it briefly.*)

It's loaded but not made ready.

(ROBERT *is delighted by this show of expertise with weapons.*)

ROBERT: Thank God, somebody who knows his job . . . I can see the point of keeping me waiting, if I'm more likely to die. Get the others done first. I can see that point totally . . .

(SURGEONS *clean the wound, removing bits of beret. The whole of the brain is exposed on* ROBERT's *left side, his scalp split, his skull opened.*)

What are you doing?

SURGEON: Cleaning it up, that's all. Bits of your beret, that sort of thing. Then we'll close it up and send you off to the *Uganda*.
ROBERT: Be warmer there. What about the pain?
SURGEON: They might give you something on the *Uganda*. See how you go . . .

> (*There is the sound of suction and irrigation of* ROBERT'S *wound. He can't see anything, but he can hear it. His eyes search upwards.*)

ROBERT: Be warmer, that's the thing. Warmer . . .

> (*More photographs are taken by an* ORDERLY.)

Int. Night. *Uganda*

The ward of the intensive-care unit of the hospital ship, at night when the steady moaning and mutterings and whimperings are at their strongest, together with the noises of the ship. Its movement, its frightening, unexplained bangings, the noises of the life-support systems, the subdued lighting all contribute to eerie and uncomfortable timelessness. ROBERT *is propped up and looking near to death, the mess of his head wound, dirt, blood, matted hair emphasized by the curious light. He is sleeping fitfully. A* NURSE *is doing the rounds of the ward with a pencil flashlight, checking pulses, looking into eyes, waking up those, like* ROBERT, *who must not be allowed to sleep too long or too deeply.*

Ext. Night. Tumbledown

ROBERT *faces his first* PRISONER; *each is terrified of the other, standing in the semi-darkness of the battle. The sounds are amazingly like the sounds on the* Uganda. ROBERT *is naked and streaming blood. The* PRISONER *approaches* ROBERT, *stumbling but getting bigger.* ROBERT *gets hold of his neck in terror.*

Int. Night. *Uganda*

The NURSE *with the flashlight is clutched at the throat by* ROBERT, *his right hand tight finger and thumb on the windpipe of the* NURSE, *whose eyes bulge and hands flap. The flashlight is dropped and rolls across the deck.* ROBERT *still has his eyes closed. He now opens them to stare at the* NURSE. *A* SECOND NURSE, *having heard the ruckus, is trying to prise* ROBERT'S *finger and thumb from the throat of the* FIRST NURSE. *He shouts for help.*
SECOND NURSE: Over here! He's crushing his windpipe!

> (*A* THIRD NURSE *comes to help. They finally manage to release the victim, who collapses.*)

Ext. Day. *Uganda*

ROBERT *opens his eyes to see the padre of the regiment,* ANGUS TOLLY, *looking at him, some shock in his eyes at the hideousness of* ROBERT'S *wound but still smiling.*

ANGUS TOLLY: Hullo, Robert, ma friend. Good news for you. There is a cease-fire. It is virtually all over, ma friend.

ROBERT: Angus! Look at who is in this ward. There is not one other platoon commander, not one. Yet this is where they should be unless they are dead. I am the only platoon commander here! The others didn't do their jobs, that's why. If they had done their jobs, they would be here or dead. Where are they? Is Hugh Mackessac dead? Is Peter Fyshe dead? Is the Noble Lord dead? There's one of my boys here – Prothero. He's worse than me. You go and talk to him, Angus. Tell him it's over.

(ROBERT *yawns and starts to cry, tears streaming down his face.* ANGUS TOLLY *tries to comfort him.*)

ANGUS TOLLY: It is all over, Robert, I assure you.

ROBERT: They won't let me sleep, Angus. Keep waking me up ... It's like ... to be honest, it's like survival training, resistance to inter-rogation, sensory deprivation, every half-hour. I don't know what day it's called ... Where *are* the others? It's failure of leadership. I'm the only platoon commander here.

ANGUS TOLLY: Today is Monday.

ROBERT: Is it? ... Good. Good. I'm glad it's over. My boys won't have to go on now without me. We've done it.

Int. Day. Long Room, Lord's

The far door is flung open and JOHN LAWRENCE *almost runs across the room, not even looking towards the pitch, where a match is in progress. He thrusts open the near door.*

Int. Day. Office, Lord's

A large man standing in the office: the COLONEL *commanding 2SG. He turns from looking out of the window as* JOHN LAWRENCE *comes in. They shake hands.* JOHN *looks at him hard; nothing is said for a moment.*

COLONEL: How much have you been told about Robert, Wing Com-mander? Do you want to sit down?

JOHN: No, I'll stand. We weren't told he was wounded even for two days. His brother, Christopher, was told there was a casualty signal, but Robert wasn't on it, then Christopher went to the battalion orderly room, saw a signal. I saw it too. Terry Knapp — dead. Robert — gunshot wound to the head. Just a nick, that's what they thought — said.

COLONEL: I'll sit down if you don't mind.

JOHN: Do.

COLONEL: He's very seriously ill, but stable, on the *Uganda*.

Int. Night. Warship *Herald*, South Atlantic

The most frightening sounds of battle: small-arms fire, machine-guns, shellfire, mortars, grenades, shouts of pain and anguish. The casualties in the small ward stare in horror and howl, some of them covering their ears, some of them cowering into the pillows. The whole ward goes berserk with terror, ROBERT *among them, on a top bunk of rows of bunks close-packed, some forty men to the ward. He stares at one of the four television screens set up in the ward in open-mouthed horror, flinching at the all too realistic film* Cross of Iron. *A* DOCTOR *storms through the ward.*

DOCTOR: Take that damn silly film off.

(ROBERT, *looking ghastly, still not cleaned up properly, very weak, is sweating with fear. The television screens go blank, and then the opening titles of* Lemon Popsicle *roll up —which is when* ROBERT *begins to relax and experiences the first movements of his bowels for several days. He groans and laughs weakly at the* PARA *underneath him.*)

ROBERT: Oh, God, watch out. I'm going to have my first shit since Tumbledown. Nurse!

PARA: Nurse, get me out of here! Nurse!

(ROBERT *laughs as a* NURSE *squeezes through the bunks.*)

Get him a bedpan! Nurse!

Int. Night. Lawrence house, Barnes

They are in their bedroom and bathroom. It is 12.30 at night. The dachshund is flat on the floor looking like a seal, eyes rolling, the way dachshunds do when they are anxious, a gentle steady whimper coming from the dog. JEAN LAWRENCE *is in bed looking very tired.* JOHN LAWRENCE *is getting ready for bed in the bathroom; he is washing.*

JEAN: Of the two boys, Christopher has taken it badly.

JOHN: Isn't it odd? He's the soldier. Nick is so calm — worried but very calm.

JEAN: Christopher probably feels it should have been him because he's the eldest, because he was in the Scots Guards before Robert ... That silly dog. Listen to him. He whimpered all night the night of the battle, didn't he? I don't believe your father heard Robert cry that night, do you?

JOHN: Yes, I do.

JEAN: Why didn't I, if he did?

> (*The telephone rings.* JOHN *is straight to it, wet hands and face, answering it at once, brusque, worried, water streaming from his hair.*)

JOHN: Yes, hello ...

> (*A loud bleep from the phone, then another, so loud that it can be heard by* JEAN.)

OPERATOR: This is wireless station Portishead. I have warship *Herald* for you ... Hold ...

> (*Bleep, then a series of bleeps and a very angry voice shouting.*)

ROBERT: Hello! Hello! Hello ...

JOHN: Hello ... Robert?

ROBERT: Have they told you what they've done to me? Hello! Hello!

> (JEAN *is now at the phone with* JOHN. *The dachshund is looking at them both from between its paws.*)

JOHN: Yes, Spud, I think I know.

ROBERT: They've blown the top of my bloody head off! Hello!

Int. Day. Warship *Herald*

ROBERT *is trying to talk into the telephone in the small radio cabin, held by a* NURSE *and a* LEADING RATING, *the four of them (including the* OPERATOR) *in a very small space.* ROBERT's *mouth is drooping; his words are slurred; his features are ghastly; and now that the excitement of using the phone is over, he is flagging. The* NURSE *is very worried about him as he talks.*

ROBERT: Look, Daddy, look ... We're going to be at Brize Norton in the morning from Montevideo tomorrow. No ... the day after ... But early ... very early, at five-thirty. Can you make it?

Int. Night. Lawrence house, Barnes

JOHN *is having the telephone taken from him by* JEAN.

JOHN: Of course we can.

(JEAN *is now also on the telephone; both hold the handset for a moment.* Then JOHN *lets go and says to her:*)

Brize Norton, tomorrow, early ... It can't be, but ...

JEAN: Hello, Robert. How are you?

ROBERT: Not very well. No ... But Brize Norton tomorrow ... It's very early ...

Int. Day. Warship *Herald*

ROBERT *is gasping. The* NURSE *takes the telephone from him as he says:*

ROBERT: Too much ... Can't talk any more ... 'Bye, Mummy.

Int. Night. Lawrence house, Barnes

JEAN *puts the telephone back.* JOHN *has gone. On the landing he blows hard into the bag of his pipes, then throws the drones over his shoulder and the starting wail is heard.* JEAN *kneels and rubs the stomach of the dachshund, which has rolled over.* JOHN *launches into a pibroch.*

Int. Day. Warship *Herald*

In the ward Lemon Popsicle *is on for the twentieth time.* ROBERT *is dressed in a strange uniform of clean combat trousers, a rating's white shirt with an anchor pinned to it and a set of Para's wings.* ROBERT *is regretting the telephone call as he is brought back into this extraordinary place, crammed with maimed and laughing men.*

ROBERT: (*VO*) I just wish I hadn't made that phone call ...

Int. Day. Kitchen of Stubbs house

HELEN, GEORGE *and* ROBERT *sit with the litter of the lunch spread over the table. There is the sound of the lavatory flush.* HUGH *has gone out of the room.*

GEORGE: Why?

ROBERT: Made me different. There was this para in the bunk underneath, a real Para Tom. He said, 'You don't want me to call you "sir" now, do ...

(*A glance at* HELEN *to make sure she hasn't taken offence.*)

... you?' I didn't. We were all the same. We were all very ill, very ill, but we were allowed to smoke, and when I went for the first time since I crapped myself on Tumbledown, it was hilarious.

(*The phone on the wall makes the 'ping' of an extension being picked up.* HELEN *looks towards it, gets up, looks worried.*)

HELEN: I don't want Hugh ringing Louise. Do you think he is?

ROBERT: Poor old Hugh. I don't know how he manages. It hasn't been easy for me, but I always was a real military shit . . . Poor Hugh, it was quite an experience for him too.

(HUGH *comes back into the kitchen.*)

HUGH: Glad you realize that, Bobbit. It wasn't all covering ourselves in glory, you know. The war didn't end when you pissed off! Some of us had to spend the rest of the day and night on that sodding mountain . . .

ROBERT: There you are. Glad I didn't.

HUGH: Your daughter isn't there, so I suppose she could be on her way.

(HELEN *and* GEORGE *exchange glances.*)

Ext. Day. Road in Oxfordshire

Pouring rain. JOHN and JEAN LAWRENCE *are driving to Brize Norton.*

Int. Day. VC10

ROBERT *looks as if he is dying. He is on a lower bunk in the VC10, and his pillow is filling up with pink fluid from his brain. His left arm is on the floor, where it keeps getting trodden on by the* STEWARD/NURSE, *who puts it back and apologizes, asking if he is all right.* ROBERT *can just manage a wan smile. The noise of the flight precludes conversation even if he were so inclined.*

Ext. Day. Brize Norton

A VC10 is arriving from Montevideo with Falklands wounded. JOHN *and* JEAN LAWRENCE *are waiting to see* ROBERT. *Other families are also waiting. A harassed* RAF OFFICER *is trying to explain to some people from Wales that their son is not on the plane.*

RAF OFFICER: I'm afraid he isn't on this one either . . .

MAN: But we've come all the way from Wales again.

RAF OFFICER: I know. I'm very sorry. As soon as we find out why, I'll let you know.

WOMAN: I don't want to know why, I just want to see my son . . .

RAF OFFICER: I'm sorry . . . Please wait here and I'll come back to you.

JOHN: Is my son on the plane?

RAF OFFICER: Yes he is, sir.

JOHN: Can we see him?

RAF OFFICER: If you wait here, I'll find out.

JEAN: But he is on it?

RAF OFFICER: Yes, Mrs Lawrence, he is.

WOMAN: This is the third time we've been. Is your son in the Welsh
Guards?

Ext. Day. Brize Norton

*The VC10 comes to the end of its taxi. A tent is pulled over the rear as
ambulances stream across the tarmac towards it.*

JEAN: (*VO*) No, he isn't. He's a Scots Guard.

Int. Day. Lounge, Brize Norton

*A television set is showing a video of some returning wounded – walking
wounded, lightly injured – all smiles and hugs and children with their fathers'
berets on.*

Ext./Int. Day. VC10 and tent

*Some very seriously injured are being taken off the plane, ROBERT among
them. The RAF NURSES take over, shocked at the sight of ROBERT but trying
not to show it. ROBERT asks weakly if his parents are there.*

RAF OFFICER: Your parents are here. They'll see you at Rawton.

(*Harassed and deeply shaken RAF MEDICAL STAFF are obviously not
prepared for the state of the wounded. Some are badly burned and
unconscious; others are feverish, crying, others are amputees, a few deathly
white, all the energy and life draining from them. The RAF MEDICAL
STAFF work quickly and silently, full of sympathy and compassion but
shaken.*)

Int. Day. Ambulance

*ROBERT is put with some others into a bus ambulance. The rain is pouring
down outside. A NURSE sits with him and holds his hand. She can't look at his
head. ROBERT manages a weak smile and tries to talk. She attempts to stop
him from talking. He begins to get angry.*

ROBERT: (*Shouting feebly*) Home! You can work it – just let them take me
home . . .

Ext. Day. Tarmac

*On crutches, angrily brushing an RAF MEDICAL ORDERLY aside, Action
Man himself, STEWART INGLIS, comes out from the tent and stands in the*

rain. He is wearing an ordinary seaman's shirt and trousers. He is looking for his wife. He sees her and stops her running towards him.

STEWART INGLIS: Get the car! Get me away from here!

Ext. Day. Road

JOHN and JEAN LAWRENCE *driving to Rawton in the pouring rain behind an ambulance.*

Int. Day. RAF Rawton

A MAN *in a wheelchair out in the lobby is shouting into the telephone, obviously in a state of great distress.*

MAN: Where were you? No good saying you weren't told I was coming. Everybody else was there. Why weren't you told? Why weren't you at Brize Norton? You must have been told. You don't bloody care. What kind of bloody woman are you?

   (*Two* COLOUR SERGEANTS, SG, *with clipboards, look for relatives as they arrive, take them to sit and wait, check names with the* RAF MEDICAL STAFF. *A* MALE NURSE *tries to take the distressed* MAN *into the ward.*)

Int. Day. Ward, RAF Rawton

NURSES *of the RAF try to make the wounded look more presentable for their relatives. Some have screens around their beds. There is a burns case which is no more than a red hole wrapped in foam on the end of a body wrapped likewise.* ROBERT *is brought in on a stretcher. Two young* NURSES *deal with him, trying to clean him up, very shocked by his wound. One of them whispers to a* NURSING OFFICER. *She comes over to check his pulse. He is still asking to be allowed to go home. This is all seen through a window. The* NURSING OFFICER *comes out to talk to an* AIR COMMODORE, *who listens to her and goes in to look at* ROBERT.

Ext. Day. RAF Rawton

JOHN and JEAN LAWRENCE *arrive with other families.*

Int. Day. Lobby, RAF Rawton

The two COLOUR SERGEANTS, SG, *are asked by* JOHN LAWRENCE *about* ROBERT. *One of them consults his clipboard; the other breaks off to talk to a very anxious* MOTHER, *who appears totally bewildered. The* AIR COM-

MODORE *comes down. He obviously knows* JOHN *and* JEAN LAWRENCE.

AIR COMMODORE: Hello, John. I've been to see Robert. Hello, Jean. We'll have to wait for a moment. They're being made comfortable. Sit down, Jean. John, let me show you where the ward is . . .

(*He takes* JOHN *to one side.* JEAN *sits bolt-upright in a chair, watching them talk.*)

Int. Day. Ward

ROBERT *is being propped up on the pillows. Some of the mess is wiped from his face. He is talking to one of the* NURSES.

ROBERT: One of your lot kept standing on my arm in the plane. Clumsy idiot. Good job I'm paralysed . . .

Int. Day. Lobby, RAF Rawton

The NURSING OFFICER *comes down into the lobby, smart, white-starched, smiling a little shakily.* JOHN *and the* AIR COMMODORE *are talking together.* JEAN, *seen beyond, is sitting very still.*

AIR COMMODORE: . . . so if he goes while you're talking to him – the girls aren't very happy about him – if he goes, do keep an eye on Jean. I'll get to you . . .

(*Families being led up the stairs to the ward,* JEAN *and* JOHN *with them.*)

Int. Day. Ward

There is laughter and the sound of a champagne bottle being opened down at the far end, where a small group is celebrating at the bedside of someone. ROBERT *is sitting up in bed, the whole of the left side of his face drooped, his mouth open slackly. When he talks his speech is very slurred because of the droop of his mouth.* JOHN *and* JEAN *appear at the bottom of the bed.* ROBERT *dissolves into tears.*

ROBERT: Daddy, it wasn't worth it!

JOHN: It was, Spud, it was . . .

(JEAN *holds his hand at the bed and just looks at him. She starts kissing his hand and puts up a hand to brush away the hair from his forehead, then stops herself.* ROBERT *is in torrents of tears.*)

ROBERT: It wasn't. They're all dead, all the boys, all my boys, all my soldiers. Prothero, Lumpy, Sergeant Brodick, Baynes, Saltemarsh – he

got it with the *Galahad*. I saved him, kiss of life, and then they got him
to the *Galahad*. All dead, Prothero, Sergeant Brodick, Lumpy. I led
them into it, basically, and it wasn't worth it ... It isn't. They're all
dead, every man in my platoon ...

JOHN: No, they're not, Spud, not at all. I've seen the casualty returns. Let
me assure you ...

ROBERT: No, no, all dead ...

JEAN: Ssssshhhh, Robert ...

ROBERT: All dead, Mummy. Prothero, Lumpy, Baynes, Richards, the
Mudges, O'Rourke. Where's Pongo? Dead.

JOHN: No, Robert. Listen to me. I know they're not dead. I'll find out. I'll
show you.

> (*He leaves the ward.* JEAN *is alone with* ROBERT.)

ROBERT: Mummy, it wasn't worth it.

JEAN: No, I know it wasn't, Robert, but you're home now.

> (*Laughter from the other side of the curtain. The ward is now full of
> wounded and relatives, some just sitting and crying, some stretched silent
> across the beds, some holding hands without saying anything. The only
> noise comes from the champagne party, which echoes and appears sadder
> than anything.* JOHN *comes back in with the two* COLOUR SERGEANTS
> SG. *They stand at the bottom of the bed and go pale at the sight of*
> ROBERT. *They both take refuge in their clipboards. One of them manages
> to speak.*)

COLOUR SERGEANT: Mr Lawrence, sorr. Your platoon state, sorr.

> (*He turns back to the clipboard.* ROBERT *has recovered, has become the
> Scots Guards officer again. He tries to put out a hand.*)

ROBERT: Colour Sergeant.

Ext. Day. RAF Rawton

JOHN *and* JEAN LAWRENCE *watch the big Chinook helicopter take off with
the wounded aboard.*

Int. Day. Chinook

R̶ ̶s to sit up. A NURSE *tightens the straps around him, murmuring

̶ ̶: regulations ...

̶ ̶ regs. Last one of these I was in, the bloody door fell

Int. Day. Wessex, Falkland Islands

The helicopter is crammed with SCOTS GUARDS. ROBERT *grabs for the door, which drops off.*

Ext. Day. RAF Rawton

JOHN *and* JEAN LAWRENCE *are walking towards their car.*

JOHN: I had a word with the pilot. He knew me. His CO was a cadet with me. You remember him . . . I told him, you take care. You've got my boy on there . . .

(*They get into the car and drive out of the hospital grounds.*)

God, I'm proud of him.

JEAN: Yes.

JOHN: 'Wasn't worth it' — did you hear him say that? He's done magnificently. I spoke to one of his boys, Fraser. He said, 'You should have seen him, sorr. He was there with two rifles, blazing away, like that film, sorr, *True Grit*. He was terrific, sorr!' God, he's done well. Hasn't he?

JEAN: Yes.

JOHN: Aren't you proud of him?

JEAN: Yes, I am.

Int. Day. Kitchen of Stubbs house

There are two very full ashtrays and three packets of Benson and Hedges cigarettes open on the table. GEORGE *is leaning forward, listening intently, while* HUGH *and* ROBERT *talk.*

HUGH: *I* had the two bloody rifles!

ROBERT: I don't know where you got them from, if you did.

(*Over this,* HELEN *is on the telephone in the hall, speaking softly to her daughter,* LOUISE.)

HELEN: You'd better not come home if you don't want to see him. I would rather you didn't anyway, Louise . . . Why? I would just rather, that's all . . . Yes. 'Bye.

(*She goes back into the kitchen.*)

Somebody else for Louise.

(ROBERT *looks at her and knows she is lying. She looks away quickly.*)

HUGH: She's bound to be here soon, isn't she?

GEORGE: I don't know, she's a law unto herself, my daughter.

ROBERT: Yes, I expect she is.

Int. Day. Military hospital

ROBERT *is a pitiable sight. He has shrunk from twelve stone and looks wasted, and his eyes are sunk deep into his skull. His hair and head are still matted with blood and dirt. The stitching of his scalp has left great black, rough stitches over the front and a gobbet of brain protruding behind. Pink fluid oozes all the time from his head. The pillow is soaked with it. His left arm is useless. His right arm has a 'manhole cover' in it, into which drips are fed. His mouth still droops to the left, so that everything he says is slurred. He has not recovered the use of his left leg, and he is incontinent. He talks a lot but can hardly be heard unless he shouts, and shouting weakens him further. All bend forward to listen to him. He is bewildered, angry, confused.* NICK, *his brother, holds his hand.* CHRISTOPHER, *his eldest brother, is furious with himself because he might cry. His face is a mixture of fury and panic that at any moment the tears may gush.* SOPHIE *is smiling.*

ROBERT: Sophie is smiling.

NICK: How are you feeling?

ROBERT: Christopher is going to cry.

CHRISTOPHER: No . . .

ROBERT: *I* do the crying. *I* do the bloody crying. Sophie, I'm going to be all right as soon as they push my brain back and stitch me up. I can't see it . . .

NICK: Yes, you're going to be all right.

ROBERT: . . . but I keep thinking it's all over the pillow, my brain . . . They won't give me anything to eat.

NICK: That's because of the operation.

ROBERT: It is all over the pillow. Look at him – he's going to cry!

CHRISTOPHER: No . . . no.

ROBERT (*Angry*) I *am* starving, you know!

SOPHIE: When you've had the op.

ROBERT: How's Daddy taking it?

NICK: Oh, you know him. Ringing everybody, everybody he was in the RAF with, to make sure you're getting everything.

ROBERT: Make sure? I wish I could have a proper piss. I can't do it properly. They won't let me smoke, you see. They WON'T! Stop smiling, Sophie. Say something.

SOPHIE: Oh, I don't know what to say really, Robert.

ROBERT: Nobody knows what to say. All right crying. What to do . . .?

38

You sent us: now *say* something . . . Nobody knows how to treat us,
NOBODY!

(ROBERT *turns away from them.*)

Int. Night. Military hospital

ROBERT *turns back to see a group of* RAMC DOCTORS *at the foot of his bed.*
CHRISTOPHER, NICK *and* SOPHIE *have gone. He has, in fact, been asleep,
and now wakes up to hear the* RAMC DOCTORS, *in their white coats over
uniform, talking about him, the classic group of self-absorbed doctors at the
patient's bedside.*

LIEUTENANT COLONEL: Gunshot wound to the head. Anyone know
what hit him?

CAPTAIN: High-velocity round of some sort.

ROBERT: Belgian FN. Seven point six two.

(*The* LIEUTENANT COLONEL *ignores* ROBERT.)

LIEUTENANT COLONEL: Anybody know what the muzzle velocity of
an FN is?

ROBERT: 40,000 feet per second. For God's sake, talk to *me* if you want
to know anything. It's my job. Bloody doctors! Talk to me!

(*The* LIEUTENANT COLONEL *rounds on* ROBERT *over the chart he is
holding and over his gold-rimmed spectacles.*)

LIEUTENANT COLONEL: Might I remind you, young man, that I am a
lieutenant colonel in the RAMC and that you are still a serving
officer? Queen's Regulations still apply to you, you know, shot or
not.

ROBERT: You . . . you can take . . .

(*The* LIEUTENANT COLONEL *has turned away again, and the group
has closed in at the bottom of the bed.* ROBERT *tries with a very weak
voice to shout.*)

. . . your rank and Queen's Regs. and you can stuff them up your
big fucking arse!

(*He turns away again in pain and frustration, saying almost as he does
so:*)

Talk to me.

(*He turns back to the sound of the news. A* NURSE *is smoothing down
the sheets and looking over her shoulders at the television screen.*)

NURSE: . . . keep us quiet. We have been shouting our mouth off at the

Senior Medical Officer, haven't we? Oh, look at those poor horses. Isn't it dreadful? Oh, look at them ...

ROBERT: Horses ... Whingeing on about the horses ... I knew him. That was a friend of mine killed in that bomb. You don't understand anything, do you?

Ext. Day. Hyde Park on TV screen

The horses of the Hyde Park bombing of the Household Cavalry are seen lying in their blood.

Int. Night. Military hospital

The right side of ROBERT'*s head has been shaved, ready for his operation in the morning. He glares at the* NURSE *and tries to grab her with his right hand, which almost tugs out the drips in his arm.*

ROBERT: You silly little bitch! Ireland ... Men were killed, blown apart. Have you seen a man blown apart? Have you?

Ext. Day. Military hospital to neurological hospital

An ambulance is being driven through the streets.

Int. Day. Ambulance

Inside the ambulance ROBERT *is in a drugged state, his mouth open, his head rolling with the movement of the ambulance. He closes his eyes.*

ROBERT: First thing they show you when you come back, friend of yours blown apart. It's still going on ... I thought it was over ... They shouldn't have shown me. They don't understand.

Int. Day. Neurological hospital

A PATIENT, *not a soldier but an elderly man, is being helped to sit up. He has a plastic bag on his head. He is given a glass of water. He throws up all over his front and whimpers.* ROBERT *opens his eyes opposite. His head is now bandaged for the first time. He groans.* MARY, *a nice Irish biddy of a nurse, clucks around him.*

MARY: There, there. How are you feeling, Robert?

ROBERT: Robert ...

MARY: That's right. Now, my name is Mary. Would you like a glass of water, dear?

ROBERT: Starving. I haven't eaten for ever such a long time.

MARY: Oh, I don't know about that. I'll have to ask doctor about that. Try some water now ...

ROBERT: Please, Mary. I'm starving ... My leg hurts, my good leg.

MARY: That's where they took a little piece of muscle, dear.

ROBERT: My good leg. I am starving.

Int. Day. John Lawrence's office, Lord's

JOHN LAWRENCE *puts down the phone, turning to* JEAN.

JOHN: Sitting up in bed eating double egg and chips.

JEAN: He's all right?

JOHN: Yes. Then he asked for more.

JEAN: Can we see him?

JOHN: Tomorrow. Where's Nick? You ring Christopher, and I'll find out where Nick is. He'll be doing a garden somewhere. Sophie ...

JEAN: Sophie is finding it very difficult with Robert.

JOHN: Why?

JEAN: She has another boyfriend.

JOHN: Has she said so?

JEAN: No, but I know she has. She has mentioned a very good friend and, well, I know. She can't find anything to say to him.

JOHN: She'll get over that. We all find it difficult.

JEAN: No, we don't, John. But she does. She isn't a bad girl. She feels awful about it, I can tell.

JOHN: I don't know. I'll go and find Nick. It's a house in Hampstead, I think ... I'll see his van parked somewhere. Then we'll go and talk to the surgeon. Do you know, he came back specially from South Africa just to do the boy's operation?

JEAN: Yes.

JOHN: I told you.

JEAN: Yes.

JOHN: Jean, you're so strong. I'm very proud of you.

(JOHN's *eyes fill with tears.*)

Ext. Day. Hampstead

NICK's *battered green-and-white van is parked.* NICK *is working with a fork, turning over a bed.* JOHN *watches him working for a moment.* NICK's *shirt hangs down over his trousers.*

41

JOHN: Double egg and chips.

NICK: Daddy, what are you talking about?

JOHN: I'm talking about Robert, Spud. Just heard. Thought I'd tell you. He came round from the operation and demanded double egg and chips at once or else, then another helping. How's that?

NICK: Great. What's he going to do, daddy?

JOHN: I don't know, Spud.

NICK: He only wants to be a soldier, you know that.

Ext. Night. Falklands

The extraordinary figure of a Scots Guardsman (BERGEN MAN) with high-piled bergen and his rifle across his body, a lumbering silhouette.

Int. Night. Neurological hospital

In the ward ROBERT opens his eyes and stirs. Giggles are coming from two NIGHT NURSES in the centre of the ward.

NIGHT NURSE 1: No way. I said, 'You put that away. I am not letting you touch me with that.'

NIGHT NURSE 2: What did he say?

NIGHT NURSE 1: What could he say? I was not having it.

NIGHT NURSE 2: I don't have the choice. I like him, though. That's something. He's a lovely man when he tries . . .

NIGHT NURSE 1: He's been trying.

NIGHT NURSE 2: I don't mind. I want to have a baby.

NIGHT NURSE 1: No way.

NIGHT NURSE 2: Oh, I don't know.

ROBERT: Nurse.

NIGHT NURSE 2: What you want?

ROBERT: Pain . . .

> (NIGHT NURSE 2 *looks at his chart. She takes his temperature and feels his pulse off-handedly.*)

I can't give you anything.

ROBERT: I know.

NIGHT NURSE 2: Then what you want?

ROBERT: Talk . . .

NIGHT NURSE 2: What about, talk?

ROBERT: Anything. I hear you're pregnant. When is it due?

NIGHT NURSE 2: You don't listen to private conversations. No way!

ROBERT: Sorry.

NIGHT NURSE 2: You keep quiet unless you are ill, and don't listen to what does not concern you. You are going to need help. You'd better start thinking about that.

ROBERT: Don't talk to me like that. I'm not one of your nut cases.

(ROBERT *is left with a glare. He reaches out for something in his locker with his right hand. One of the* NIGHT NURSES *is smoking, the cigarette held in a cupped hand with the furtive expertise of long practice.*)

NIGHT NURSE 2: Cheeky sod. He asked me when I'm due.

NIGHT NURSE 1: How does he know?

NIGHT NURSE 2: Just listening to private conversations, that's how.

(*A flicker of light beyond as* ROBERT *clicks his cigarette lighter. It is not noticed at once.* ROBERT *is holding the flame of his lighter to his left hand. Now it is noticed.*)

No smoking!

NIGHT NURSE 1: Stop him!

(*As one of the* NIGHT NURSES *bustles over to* ROBERT, *he falls out of bed with the effort of reaching over to his left. The whole of the left side of his body collapses, and he is gone.*)

Int. Night. Neurological hospital

A tubby, round-faced, north-country YOUNG DOCTOR, *wearing small, metal-rimmed glasses, is hurrying through the corridor of the grotty old hospital, his bleeper going. He is bursting out of a too-small white coat and has trouble with his bleeper.*

Int. Night. Neurological hospital

The two NIGHT NURSES *have got* ROBERT *back into bed. The* YOUNG DOCTOR *examines him, shining a flashlight in his eyes and feeling his pulse.*

NIGHT NURSE 1: He was smoking, doctor.

YOUNG DOCTOR: All right, nurse.

NIGHT NURSE 2: Could have blown us all up. There's oxygen on the ward.

YOUNG DOCTOR: All right, I can manage. Motorbike?

ROBERT: What?

YOUNG DOCTOR: Come off your bike, did you?

ROBERT: Sort of ... No, Falklands.

43

YOUNG DOCTOR: Ah, you're one.

(*The* YOUNG DOCTOR, *sympathetic, grins and finishes his examination.*)
I expect you know all about it, blowing people up?

ROBERT: A bit. I just wanted to talk to them, silly cows. I wasn't
smoking actually, though . . .

YOUNG DOCTOR: Not in here. It really is dangerous, and half these
people are in comas. We'd never get them out if we had a fire.

ROBERT: I was seeing if I had any feeling in my left hand. I did it first on
the *Uganda*, but that was weeks ago . . . Do you drive?

YOUNG DOCTOR: Of course.

ROBERT: What?

YOUNG DOCTOR: A beaten up old MG.

ROBERT: That's all right. I feel if I can get in a car, I'll be able to use the
gear lever. Do you know what I mean? I felt that on the *Uganda*.

YOUNG DOCTOR: Do you fancy a beer?

ROBERT: Is that all right?

YOUNG DOCTOR: I'll get them in. Wait there till I come back.

(*The* YOUNG DOCTOR *goes.* ROBERT *grins, lies back and closes his
eyes.*)

Int. Day. Neurological hospital

ROBERT *wakes up. A can of beer is on his locker.* MARY *is fussing round his
bed, taking his pulse, temperature, putting the can of beer away, straightening
the sheets.*

MARY: How are we this morning, Robert? I've heard about your adven-
tures in the night — what a naughty boy you are! And for your
information, young man, they are *not* nut cases.

(ROBERT *looks around the ward. Almost all the* PATIENTS *are in comas
and have to be turned.*)

They are fellow neurological patients, however much they look like
nut cases.

ROBERT: I'm dying for a cigarette.

MARY: Then you'll have to die because you can't smoke in here. You
must wait until we can get you into a wheelchair . . . First of all you'll
have to learn to sit up. Look at you, all slumped over. Physios for you.

Ext. Night. Falklands

The lumbering BERGEN MAN, *again with his bergen piled high and his rifle*

44

across his chest, puts one foot laboriously in front of the other, teetering, settling back, then forward again, slow, in mist and snow wipe.
ROBERT: (*VO*) Do you know what a high-velocity bullet does?

Int. Night. Neurological hospital

The YOUNG DOCTOR *is sitting with* ROBERT, *holding a can of beer. The* NIGHT NURSES *are in the background, glowering.*
YOUNG DOCTOR: No. Hurts?
ROBERT: It does that.

Ext. Day. Sandhurst

A group of OFFICER CADETS *in combat dress, among them* ROBERT, *are being given a demonstration of the effect of ammunition. A* SERGEANT *fires several rounds of low-velocity ammunition into a large oil drum, and water spurts from the holes. Then he fires a high-velocity round from a self-loading rifle and the oil drum empties in a rush from the top.*

Int. Night. Neurological hospital

ROBERT: Not a drop left in it. One round and *whoosh*, out of the top.
YOUNG DOCTOR: Bloody hell.
ROBERT: Quite. Imagine a brain.
YOUNG DOCTOR: What are you going to do?
ROBERT: Go back and pick up the bits?
YOUNG DOCTOR: No, when you're fit. Thought about it?
ROBERT: How fit am I going to be?
YOUNG DOCTOR: Haven't you seen your surgeon?
ROBERT: Yes, but you tell me.
YOUNG DOCTOR: Do you want me to? Paralysed down the left side, complete. You'll regain some functioning. Might be able to do without that catheter. Might be able to control your bowels. Your mouth will perhaps straighten, become a smile rather than a leer. But you'll never be able to use your left hand or arm or leg. You'll never walk — properly that is. You took your last real walk on the Falklands, Robert.
ROBERT: That's what he said. Piss off!
YOUNG DOCTOR: You'll have to learn to be nicer to doctors and nurses. You're going to see a lot of them.
ROBERT: I said, piss off.
 (*The* YOUNG DOCTOR *looks at his watch and does.*)

Int. Day. Physiotherapy unit

The HOSPITAL CHAPLAIN *is on his rounds, smiling, popping his head round doors.*

CHAPLAIN: Morning, nurse. Morning, Auntie. Morning, Mr Edwards. That's right. How are we this morning?

> (ROBERT *with two girls,* ANGIE *and* TRICIA, *who are physiotherapists, making heavy weather of trying to sit in a wheelchair. The* CHAPLAIN *is heard over, greeting the elderly people recovering from strokes and pressure on the brain. Paternalism is rampant.*)

ROBERT: I can't sit straight.

TRICIA: Try, there's a good boy. He can do it, can't he, Angie?

ANGIE: He can, Tricia. He doesn't know what he can do until he tries, does he?

TRICIA: That's right. Put more weight on your right buttock . . . That's right.

ANGIE: You're slipping! You're slipping!

ROBERT: Of course I'm bloody slipping. There's nothing there. It's like leaning against a trick wall.

ANGIE: Don't swear. We can do it.

ROBERT: I'm *doing* it. Don't call me 'boy'.

> (TRICIA *has had enough. She wheels the chair past the* CHAPLAIN *into a very small room, followed by* ANGIE.)

TRICIA: Let's see what we look like, shall we?

> (*There is a full-length mirror in the room.* ROBERT *is shoved up against it, very close, and then pulled back so that he can see himself. It is the first time he has seen himself drooping over to the left, dribble running from the left side of a drooping mouth, left arm and leg useless, eyes sunk deep into his head. He screams at them for what he sees as their cruelty.*)

ROBERT: What do you know, you two? What do you know? Do you know what it's like to kill someone? Bits come off them. Bits . . . They don't die all at once, like the television. They keep coming at you, and lumps fly off them. You don't know that, do you?

> (*The* CHAPLAIN *stands in the doorway, transfixed.* ANGIE *and* TRICIA *are shocked at* ROBERT's *fury.*)

Bits blown off. You see it! I've done that. I've done that! Look at me.

CHAPLAIN: Thank you, young man. I was privileged to hear that compassionate outburst.

ROBERT: It isn't that. You stab and you keep on stabbing. You don't know how much it takes to kill a squirming man!

(*Left alone*, ROBERT *glares at the wreck he has become in the mirror.*)

(*VO*) Look, I want you to tell that idiot. It's my right side . . .

Int. Night. Neurological hospital

The YOUNG DOCTOR *and* ROBERT *are chatting.*

YOUNG DOCTOR: Why?

ROBERT: Then at the end of the service he'll get a shock when I shove out my right hand to shake hands . . . God, what an idiot. I hate him.

Int. Day. Chapel

ROBERT *wheeled forward, the* CHAPLAIN *putting his hands on his head and giving his blessing,* ROBERT *looking at him and hating him.*

ROBERT: (*VO*) I'll be able to drive eventually, won't I?

Int. Night. Neurological hospital

Giggling NIGHT NURSES *are in the background as the* YOUNG DOCTOR *sits with* ROBERT.

YOUNG DOCTOR: I don't know.

ROBERT: Surely automatic? That's the only thing I must be able to do, the only thing I care about.

Ext. Night. Falklands

BERGEN MAN *sways first one way and then the other, lost in the mists of the Falklands.*

YOUNG DOCTOR: (*VO*) Had any more letters?

ROBERT: (*VO*) Mad Dog – O'Rourke, called Mad Dog – he's written. One of my soldiers.

Int. Night. Neurological hospital

ROBERT *reads the letter from* O'ROURKE.

ROBERT: 'I was one of the lucky ones to guard the spics at Ajax Bay, and although none of which claimed to have anything to do with Tumbledown, the boys really messed them around, they didn't sleep much, and if you were to ask the Noble Lord, he'd verify our general nastiness to them, much to his enjoyment, I'm glad to say. Well, sir, you've not missed anything. Everything we've done since Tumble-down has been really boring . . .'

Int. Day. Kitchen of Stubbs house

GEORGE *and* ROBERT *are talking, still seated at the table.*

GEORGE: Did you see any others while you were in hospital? Did you look them up?

ROBERT: Why?

GEORGE: Weren't they with you?

ROBERT: To be honest, I didn't give a damn about anyone else. Only cared about myself. Do you know what it's like? You try going about all day with your left hand tied to your body, all day . . . Look at my shoes. I couldn't get anyone to tie my laces this morning. Look . . . Hugh was going to . . . Look, it's the confusion bugs me. One minute allowed to smoke, the next not . . . One minute I can drive, then I am driving, then not . . . One minute an officer in one of the elite regiments of the world, a history going back centuries, next a dribbling in-continent, told off by silly little night nurses who only want to talk about their sex lives – how they've got one, how they're getting one, how they can keep it up, man . . .

Ext. Night. Falklands

BERGEN MAN, *confused, sways out of the mists. Music, tinny: guitar, sitar.*

Int. Day. Military hospital, Robert's room

ROBERT *has been transferred to the military hospital. His bandages are off. His scar is still livid, the hair just growing over it. His Sony Walkman on, he is listening to the Corries:* 'Hush a babe while the red bee hums . . .' *On his locker and on tables are cards from well-wishers, a television set, a video, a coffee percolator, a radio, a digital alarm, a stereo and a personal computer. The door is just closing on someone.*

Int. Day. Military hospital corridor

The entourage of a civilian Very Important Person is going into the room next to ROBERT'S.

Int. Day. Military hospital, CSM Brown's room

CSM BROWN *has a wounded hand. He holds it behind his back and greets the VIP coolly.*

CSM BROWN: Good afternoon, sir. I thought you had resigned.

Int. Day. Military hospital, Robert's room

CSM BROWN *is standing in the doorway.* ROBERT *has switched his Sony Walkman off.*

ROBERT: He couldn't look at my head, Company Sergeant-Major. All he could say was what a lot of cards I had. He didn't want to talk about the war, anything . . .

CSM BROWN: Precisely the same with me, sir. Bloody visitors. Why don't they leave us alone? They love it, sir, love it, the bastards. Have you had the Families Officer, sir?

ROBERT: I've had everyone.

CSM BROWN: And me. Went right through my hand, you know. If my rifle had not been there, it would have gone into a very vital part. You all right that way, sir?

ROBERT: Don't know, Company Sergeant-Major. Haven't tested it yet.

CSM BROWN: Let me know soon as you have won't you, sir? I shall be agog. Less to the point, it would have killed me. (*With great satisfaction*) I said to him, 'Good afternoon, sir. I thought you'd resigned.' Had your whisky from the Prince of Wales, I see.

(MAJOR NEWMAN, *an officer in Queen Alexandra's Royal Army Nursing Corps, comes into the room. She is tall, dark and attractive in a severe way.*)

MAJOR NEWMAN: Sergeant-Major Brown?

CSM BROWN: Ma'am. Mr Lawrence was talking about escaping, ma'am. Forced to tell you.

MAJOR NEWMAN: It'll be a long time before Mr Lawrence escapes.

(CSM BROWN *goes.* MAJOR NEWMAN *takes* ROBERT'S *pulse, looking down at him.*)

How do you feel, Robert?

ROBERT: Bored.

MAJOR NEWMAN: What did he say to you?

ROBERT: What lovely cards.

MAJOR NEWMAN: Aren't they?

ROBERT: You don't frighten me, Major Newman.

MAJOR NEWMAN: Nor you I, Robert. Do you want something to read?

ROBERT: I'm not a reader.

MAJOR NEWMAN: Where did you go to school?

ROBERT: Fettes. They kicked me out.

MAJOR NEWMAN: I thought all you Guards officers were Eton.

ROBERT: I'm different. Had a letter from my old headmaster saying he was proud of me. That's what comes of being shot in the head.

MAJOR NEWMAN: How are you getting on in physio?

ROBERT: I can nearly sit.

MAJOR NEWMAN: You'll manage it. But take your time – you are still very ill.

ROBERT: Don't I look it?

MAJOR NEWMAN: Yes, you do. What did the Duke of Kent say to you?

ROBERT: He had a cup of coffee. We talked. He told his lot to stay outside.

MAJOR NEWMAN: Yes, so I hear. Is that all?

ROBERT: Oh we talked about the Falklands.

MAJOR NEWMAN: You don't talk about it.

ROBERT: To you I don't.

MAJOR NEWMAN: I'd listen if you wanted to.

ROBERT: I don't. Sometimes I want to talk and can't stop. Sometimes I don't ever want to utter another word. Look.

(ROBERT *punches up his computer. On the screen is an elaborate assessment of the chances of 'escape' from the hospital.*)

MAJOR NEWMAN: What is it?

(*She has to put glasses on to see.*)

How silly.

ROBERT: What would we talk about if we talked? Yomping? That's all anybody seems to want to know about it. That's all that will ever be remembered about it. We don't know anything about yomping. We didn't yomp. We weren't strange characters who yomped. Before Tumbledown I talked to a Para who said all we had to do was bang away with an 84-mm rocket launcher and the Argies would run. Well, they didn't, not the Argies we met. They stuck. I'm one of the few soldiers in this hospital who is here because he did what he is supposed to do. Aren't I? Died for Queen and Country. Eh?

(ROBERT *puts his Sony Walkman on. He closes his eyes.*)

Ext. Night. Falklands

BERGEN MAN *is doing his slow walking to streams of tracer in the night. The strange sitar/guitar music is heard over.*

Int. Night. Military hospital, Prothero's room

MRS PROTHERO *is sitting at the bedside, her hair a mass of spikes colours, her mascara running as she gently weeps.* PROTHERO's *big hand, tattooed with H.A.T.E., holds her finger with her wedding and engagement rings on it, one of his fingers rubbing the rings. He is stretched flat on the bed, a wasted sight, tubes going into his mouth and into his stomach, bags draining off his fluids, drips draining into him. He has become a moaning, wasted shadow of his former skinhead toughness and pride.* ROBERT *wheels himself into the room with difficulty.*

ROBERT: I still can't steer straight, Pongo.

PROTHERO: Aye. Meet the wife, sir.

ROBERT: Hello, Mrs Prothero. How is he?

MRS PROTHERO: I think he's going to die. It's terrible.

ROBERT: It is. Hey, Pongo, you're not going to die.

PROTHERO: I would to spite the buggers.

ROBERT: God, isn't it awful!

Int. Day. Military hospital

ROBERT, *looking awful, sweating with the effort, wheels himself along the corridor from a lift which has brought him down. He has a small holdall on his knees. A gaggle of* NURSES *walks past him. One of them recognizes him.*

NURSE: Are you leaving us, Mr Lawrence?

ROBERT: (*Under his breath*) Bloody am.

Ext. Day. Outside the military hospital

A taxi arrives. The CABBY *gets out and* ROBERT *waves to him.*

Int. Day. Outside the military hospital

ROBERT *is being helped into the taxi.*

ROBERT: Will you put my wheelchair into the front if it will go?
    (ROBERT *is looking ghastly, still with a drip in his arm. He flops on to the seat.*)

CABBY: No trouble there, sir. Made for wheelchairs . . .
    (*The* CABBY *packs the wheelchair and gets in behind the wheel.*)
  Where to, sir?

ROBERT: King's Road. Anywhere will do.

Ext. Day. Taxi in traffic

The cab is held up at traffic lights, then there is a snarl-up as somebody cuts across the taxi and the CABBY *shouts at him. Then to* ROBERT:

CABBY: They'll never learn, will they, sir, know what I mean? There wasn't room there. Thoughtless, know what I mean? No thought for other road users. I make my living at it, know what I mean? I can't afford to risk my life.

(*He looks in his mirror at* ROBERT.)

(*Cheerfully*) You look as if you've been in the wars, sir.

(ROBERT *starts to laugh, and the* CABBY *joins him.*)

(*Slightly bewildered*) Have I said something? Eh? No, go on ... eh? Because I don't mean to, know what I mean, eh?

(ROBERT *is almost helpless with laughter.*)

Eh? No, straight up ... eh?

ROBERT: Right ... Yes, I have been in the wars. They've let me out for the day, though.

(*The* CABBY, *still bewildered, compounds it all.*)

CABBY: Well, that's something isn't it? Know what I mean? Can't win 'em all, eh?

(*Further bewilderment as he sees* ROBERT's *reaction to this in his mirror.*)

Ext. Day. King's Road

ROBERT *is in his wheelchair, trying to push himself along the King's Road, sweat pouring from him, his mouth drooping, his left arm and leg jerking with clonus. He stops in a state of terror, looking about him at the traffic and the curious faces.* HENRIETTA *sees him from the other side of the road.*

ROBERT: Oh, Christ!

HENRIETTA: Robert!

(HENRIETTA *crosses the road to him.*)

You look awful, Robert. Isn't anybody with you? Where are you going?

ROBERT: Nowhere. Just ... take me to Sophie.

HENRIETTA: No. She's not there, Robert.

ROBERT: Ring my father, will you?

HENRIETTA: I'd better take you back to the flat.

(*She pushes* ROBERT *across the road.*)

Int. Day. Military hospital, Prothero's room

PROTHERO *is lying on his bed, looking like death.* FRASER *nudges him.*

FRASER: Hey, Pongo, the boss has bugged off!

PROTHERO: Who?

FRASER: Mr Lawrence. He's went and split.

PROTHERO: Whoo! Maybe he'll get to waste a few heads along the way.

FRASER: He didnae even wait to tak his tubes oot. Wrapped they round his fuckin' neck and went. *True Grit*. Am I right or wrong?

PROTHERO: You're right!

Int. Day. John Lawrence's car

JOHN, *furious, is driving very badly in his anger.* ROBERT *is looking like death.*

ROBERT: I just thought I'd see Sophie . . . a few of the old haunts . . .

JOHN: I rang them, Spud. They didn't know you were even gone. They should never have let you out of the gates. For heaven's sake, it's a military hospital.

ROBERT: I should never have let them have me. Like Stewart Inglis, I should have got in the car at Brize Norton. I bet he even drove it.

JOHN: Are you all right?

ROBERT: Yes, I'm all right.

JOHN: I won't tell your mother.

ROBERT: Don't, daddy.

Int. Day. Military hospital, Robert's room

ROBERT *is wheeled into his room and put to bed.* MAJOR NEWMAN *is furious.* JOHN LAWRENCE *is furious.*

JOHN: I would never say this in front of Robert, but this is very bad security. If anybody can get out, then anybody can get in.

MAJOR NEWMAN: That's right, Wing Commander, and I will not let it happen again.

Int. Day. Military hospital, Robert's room

ROBERT *is in bed, and* NURSES *are cleaning him up. He has wet himself among other things.*

MAJOR NEWMAN: You are very stupid. You are still dangerously ill. You could haemorrhage. You could go into convulsions. Your brain is protected only by a thin layer of skin and part of the muscle of your own leg. There is still danger of infection, which could kill you or at best send you into a coma for life. You could have an epileptic fit. If you have one, you will have another. If you have two, you are more than likely to have more. Every day that you do not have a fit there is less chance you will have one, which is why you must be kept quiet and in a hospital.

(*She feels his pulse.* ROBERT, *as angry as she, glares at her, then raves at her.*)

ROBERT: There is no way you are going to tell me off! No way!

Ext. Night. Falklands

BERGEN MAN *runs with the towering bergen on his back, stumbling, sliding, twisting in confusion. Music.*

Int. Day. St Paul's Cathedral

The sound of the organ rises in the almost empty church. ROBERT *is wheeled to a place at the side by one of the two* COLOUR SERGEANTS SG *seen at Rawton.* ROBERT *is not in uniform and looks dreadful. His hair is just starting to grow but is longer on one side than the other. He sits and shivers, almost alone. One or two other wounded are brought in. Scaffolding for television cameras is near; cables are run. The cameras are directed down the nave, where the bulk of the congregation for the Falkland Islands Service will sit an hour from now.*

Int. Day. Gym

ROBERT *is lying on the floor.* BENNY CODRINGTON, *a black physiotherapist, is lifting* ROBERT's *left knee up and trying to get him to hold it in place, but it keeps flopping over.*

BENNY: Stay up there.

ROBERT: I am trying.

BENNY: It's going to take a long time.

ROBERT: Look at it.

BENNY: Come on — use the other side of your body. Control it from the other side.

(ROBERT, *exasperated, shouts as his knee flops over again.*)

ROBERT: Don't tell me what to do!

BENNY: You ought to be able to keep it up, wooden-top. Young wooden-top like you ...

(ELDERLY LADIES *look away as* ROBERT *sweats and struggles and rages to keep his knee up.*)

ROBERT: Look at the sodding useless thing.

(BENNY *lies down on the floor with him, provoking him.*)

BENNY: You need a good physiotherapist — *sir.*

ROBERT: Physiotherapist! Physioterrorist! I waste terrorists.

54

BENNY: When you can find them, soldier boy. Relax. Relax. You want to waste something? Waste this then.

(BENNY *seizes* ROBERT's *left arm and stretches it, rubbing it down its length, grinning evilly at* ROBERT's *pain.*)

ROBERT: You shit. You . . .

BENNY: Say it. Open the box. What's this, man? What's this? You're paralysed, man. You can't feel it!

ROBERT: I bloody can. The rest of me can.

BENNY: Hey, these Guards — are they rubbish?

ROBERT: You wouldn't say that if I was ramming a grenade down your throat, you . . .

BENNY: Say it!

ROBERT: Sorry, got to go.

BENNY: Okay, okay. Here, soldier, piss in this.

Int. Day. St Paul's Cathedral

The cathedral is gradually filling up. The seats are arranged for guests, cordoned off. There is the flutter of a helicopter outside. ROBERT *is sitting slumped in his wheelchair, waiting.*

Int. Day. Military hospital, Prothero's room

PROTHERO *is lying in bed with the door to his room open. The television set in the ward is on.* FRASER *is with* PROTHERO. *On the screen the guests are seen arriving at St Paul's Cathedral. A very low-key service is about to begin. The cameras roaming over the nave, which has filled up.*

Int. Day. St Paul's Cathedral

The COLOUR SERGEANT *leans over* ROBERT.

COLOUR SERGEANT: All right, sorr? Aye?

ROBERT: Yes, Colour Sergeant.

Int. Day. Military hospital

ROBERT, *with his hands held on front of him, tries to get up from his wheelchair, still flopping over to the left.*

BENNY: Come on. Know what the Paras call the Guards? Craphats. Am I right? Yomp! Yomp! Let's see you yomp.

ROBERT: Yomp off, you . . .

BENNY: Say it! Open the box!

Int. Day. St Paul's Cathedral

Everybody is there, but no one is seen. A voice is heard reading the Sermon on the Mount. ROBERT'S *left leg goes into spasm. The* COLOUR SERGEANT *leans over him again.*

ROBERT: It's all right, Colour Sergeant. It's called clonus. It doesn't mean it works; it means it *wants* to.

> (ROBERT *can't be seen and can't see a thing. The nearby television cameras are concentrating on the nave and the principals.*)

Int. Day. Military hospital, ward

A television set is on in the ward. FRASER *is watching it.* PROTHERO *can be seen through the door. The hymn 'All my hope on God is founded' can be heard.*

Int. Day. St Paul's Cathedral

ROBERT *is trying to sing, the hymn sheet held in his shaking right hand. A tablet inscribed 'Lieutenant Reper, HM 28th Regt. Died of wounds . . .' is directly in his line of vision. The congregation is singing the hymn: 'Sword and Crown betray his trust . . .'*

Ext. Day. St Paul's Cathedral

POLICE *on scaffolding around the outside of the cathedral look intently through their binoculars. The flutter of the helicopter creates a distraction. The first notes of a bugle are heard below in the cathedral.*

Ext. Night. Falklands

BERGEN MAN *stands stock-still, then slowly turns like the head of a giant beast. There is strange guitar/sitar music on the wind for just a second.*

Int. Day. St Paul's Cathedral

ROBERT, *deeply affected by the sounding of the Last Post, is seen through the viewfinder of a camera, reflected upside-down, Then right way up as he pushes his hand to his cheek. He is sitting hunched under the scaffolding. Reveille is being played.*

Int. Night. Military hospital, Robert's room

There is a photograph of SOPHIE *on* ROBERT'S *locker.* ROBERT, *in bed, leans over to indicate the photograph and, as if seeing it for the first time, dissembles.*

ROBERT: Oh, that! My sister-in-law, you know. Sister-in-law? The person married to my brother . . .

(*A stunningly beautiful blonde Swedish girl,* INGRID, *very young, who doesn't speak English very well, sits on the other side of the bed. Some magazines that she has brought are on the coverlet; they are Swedish and pornographic.*)

INGRID: Yes?

ROBERT: Yes. But I am not of any use to you any more. You have come a long way for nothing. We did not have much to say to each other, did we?

INGRID: I go to Embassy in Sweden, uh, and they tell me, uh, and I come . . . here . . . Robert, I older now am.

ROBERT: Yes.

INGRID: Read.

(ROBERT *is nonplussed.* INGRID *slides her hand under the coverlet.*)

Int. Day. St Paul's Cathedral

The cathedral is nearly empty now, but ROBERT *is still there. The* COLOUR SERGEANT *looks at his watch.*

Int. Night. Military hospital, Robert's room

INGRID *is just seen leaving* ROBERT, *her hand waving round the door.*

ROBERT: Well done, Ingrid.

Int. Day. St Paul's Cathedral

The cathedral is absolutely empty now except for ROBERT *and a few others in wheelchairs. The* COLOUR SERGEANT *is fussing about, not knowing what to do.*

ROBERT: Come on, Colour Sergeant. Get me out of here.

COLOUR SERGEANT: Sorr, just the wait, now . . .

ROBERT: Two hours. I've been sitting here two hours, Colour Sergeant. Couldn't see anything. Couldn't be seen. Couldn't wear uniform. What are they frightened of?

(ROBERT *tries to wheel his chair away from the wall but gets tangled in the cables and scaffolding.*)

Come on, Colour Sergeant. Get us out.

Int. Night. Military hospital, Robert's room

On the television screen the service is on The Nine O'Clock News. ROBERT *is sitting up in bed as the Last Post is sounded, once again deeply affected. Then, to his shock, he sees himself, hears hushed tones.*

COMMENTATOR: ... and in pride of place at the service was Lieutenant Robert Lawrence of the Scots Guards, severely wounded at Tumbledown ...

Int. Day. St Paul's Crypt

ROBERT *being taken out through the crypt by the* COLOUR SERGEANT, *his voice echoing. Other wounded in wheelchairs are with him.*

ROBERT: It's as if we shouldn't have come back or something ...

Int. Night. Military hospital, Robert's room

ROBERT *gets out of bed, holds on to the bed and tries to walk ...*

Ext. Night. Falklands

... As does BERGEN MAN.

Int. Night. Military hospital, Robert's room

ROBERT, *holding his hands together, tries to stand, then tries to walk and falls.*

Int. Day. Gym

ROBERT, *standing up from his wheelchair, screams at* BENNY.

ROBERT: Walk! Get me to walk, Benny! I'm going to march in a parade, in uniform, with medals, and show them this ... My head. I'm proud of it.

    (BENNY *grins, almost sadistically, it seems.*)

BENNY: And how are you going to do that, soldier?

ROBERT: Benny, please.

BENNY: All right, Robert, let's consider it. You can't use parallel bars because you have no way of supporting yourself on the left. You can't use crutches for the same reason. A walking stick, yes, but you're a Guards officer. How would you raise your hat to a lady? Now, hands clasped. That's a start. Left foot, right foot ... Oh, man, you do look a mess.

    (ROBERT's *left hand starts to shake with clonus.* BENNY *grabs it and shoves it down the front of* ROBERT's *tracksuit.*)

Never waste anything, Robert. Life's too short — too short to be caught short.

Int. Night. Medical school, lecture room

A slide of a high-velocity exit wound in the upper part of an arm. LIEU-
TENANT-COLONEL TAUNTON *is lecturing on 'Medical Aspects of the
Falklands Campaign' to Merton Medical Society. Present as a guest is* JOHN
LAWRENCE.

TAUNTON: Note the tattoo — rather an artistic effort — just below the
exit wound. We thought he would hate to lose it, and he didn't as you
can see from this photograph (*slide of the arm and the tattoo*) some
months later . . .

Int. Night. Outside the lecture room

*The title of the lecture is seen. Applause is heard from inside the lecture room.
The audience comes out, among them* JOHN LAWRENCE, *who is called
back by the organizer,* DR JESSOPS, *to meet* TAUNTON. *They shake
hands.*

TAUNTON: I heard you might be here. I have some photographs of
Robert's wound. Would you like copies?
JOHN: Yes. Thank you.
TAUNTON: They might be disturbing.
JOHN: I think my son would like to have them.

Ext. Day. Military hospital

CHRISTOPHER *and* NICK *are with* ROBERT, *who is walking very slowly.*
NICK *is ready with the wheelchair, but nevertheless* ROBERT *is managing.*

ROBERT: Where are we going?
CHRISTOPHER: Thought we'd take you to Sophie.
NICK: Are you all right, Robert?
ROBERT: Now.
    (NICK *shoves the wheelchair under* ROBERT, *who drops into it.*)
    That wasn't bad, was it?
NICK: Great.
ROBERT: What does Sophie think?
CHRISTOPHER: She doesn't know . . .
    (ROBERT *gets into the car, and* NICK *stows the wheelchair.*)
ROBERT: Can I drive?
CHRISTOPHER: No, you can't. It's a new car. I wouldn't let you drive it
anyway.

Int. Night. Sophie's flat

SOPHIE *opens the door to see* ROBERT *standing there.*

Int. Night. Bedroom, Sophie's flat

ROBERT *and* SOPHIE *are in bed.*

SOPHIE: I knew you could do it.

ROBERT: Yes. I knew.

SOPHIE: What about dancing?

ROBERT: That's going to be a fairly interesting spectacle.

SOPHIE: Robert, it doesn't matter, but you never did like balls and things, did you, ever?

ROBERT: Not much. Why, have you accepted an invitation?

SOPHIE: No, but I mean I do, actually, very much. And you're so down on people with money, aren't you?

ROBERT: Well, I've slogged for everything I have. My parents don't support me.

SOPHIE: No.

> (*The telephone rings.* SOPHIE *gets up to answer it. She answers it in such an excited way that it is obvious to* ROBERT *it is somebody more important to her than he is.*)

Hello! Gosh, yes. How nice ... Really? No, sorry ... No ... Yes ... Yes, Robert. Yes, that Robert. He's staying the night ... Yes, isn't that nice?

> (SOPHIE *puts the phone down.*)

Robert, that's the last time. I am very fond of you. But, Robert ... it's everything else ... now. What will you do?

ROBERT: When?

SOPHIE: When it happens again.

ROBERT: When I meet somebody, you mean?

SOPHIE: Somebody else ... yes.

ROBERT: I don't know. Tell them, I suppose, from the beginning, before they take me on – the shakes, the rest of it. And I do get bloody angry about things. Tell them. Soon as I know just what I am going to be. All of it. I hate you at the moment. I won't hit you, but I do hate you.

SOPHIE: Yes, I'm sure you do. Sorry.

ROBERT: That's all right.

SOPHIE: If I still loved you or anything, it would be different – do you see what I mean? – I suppose.

ROBERT: I hope so.

SOPHIE: One can't get away from the fact, you are a different person. I mean, not just your injury, but that of course . . . I mean, it terrifies me to think of living with you. We weren't, after all, going to marry or anything, were we? We hadn't seen each other for weeks before you went down there.

ROBERT: Yes, all right. Look, I've made a mess in the bed . . . Hope you don't expect me to apologize. It happens.

Ext. Day. Country road

JEAN LAWRENCE *is driving the car.* ROBERT *is with her in the front seat.*

ROBERT: I'm sure I'll be able to drive soon.

JEAN: Of course.

ROBERT: I mean, there's nothing to stop me, basically, is there? I've got a driving licence. Somewhere. I took the bloody thing to the Falklands. Don't know why. Nothing to drive there . . .

JEAN: Robert, you can't walk properly yet.

ROBERT: Precisely why I need to be able to drive. I'll get Nick to take me out in the garden van . . .

JEAN: You won't!

Int. Day. Military Hospital rehabilitation unit

A Nissen hut: there are some beds with rolled mattresses, one of them, in the far corner of the room, occupied by an OLD MAN *wearing a dressing-gown. In the centre of the room is a plastic-topped table with a sauce bottle on it.* JEAN LAWRENCE *wheels* ROBERT *into the hut. They look at it, aghast.*

JEAN: This is awful.

ROBERT: Isn't it? One thing after another, so much so it seems funny. If it's not one thing, it's another. When we were packing to go to the Falklands, one thing after another, more and more to go into our packs, hilarious, on to our backs, stuffed into our packs, everything in and still more to go in, so that we were loaded like pack mules. Towering up on our backs, huge loads that exhausted you after a mile. Fall down, you couldn't get up without help. Those bloody bergens, they're still finding something else to stuff in them . . .

(JEAN *has gone.* ROBERT *sits staring at the sauce bottle, shrunk, dejected again, shaking his head, slumping down to the left, his face drooped.*)

OLD MAN: There's no smoking in here you know, no smoking . . .

ROBERT: (*Roars*) I'm an officer in the Scots Guards, you silly old fart!

Mix to:
Ext. Night. Falklands

BERGEN MAN *sways and stumbles.*

Mix to:
Int. Day. Office, Lord's

JOHN LAWRENCE *picks up the phone promptly and listens.*
JOHN: Just stay there with him, Jean. I'm coming.

Int. Day. Military Hospital, ward

ROBERT, FRASER, PROTHERO *are sitting close together, a tight, disgruntled huddle, so that we can hear what they are saying but can't see them talking.*
ROBERT, FRASER, PROTHERO: This bleeding South Atlantic Fund, you see any of it, sir? No. Pongo, you? Nar, not a bleedin' penny. What you going to do with it, Pongo? Stingray, eh? Pension, that's something, sorr. Families Officer been round? Him! Can't get no sense out of him, boss — pensions, anything. The Fund. They don't know. They just sit and look at you. Think they hadn't never seen tubes before. Do home brewing, don't they? Ask them if you're still in the Army, they don't know. Ask them if you're not, they don't bleeding know. Aye, still in the Guards, they don't know. You, sorr? I don't know any more than you. Officers are supposed to look after themselves Officers! Not you, sorr! Only thing I've ever wanted to do, soldier. Right.

Mix to:
Ext Night. Falklands

BERGEN MAN, *confused, stumbles, searches in the mist, goes down.*
PROTHERO: (*VO*) Up until the day you leave, they hope you'll get better. After that, they're worried that you will, right, sir?

Mix to:
Int. Day. Nissen hut

ROBERT *is sitting on the bed, shaking.* JEAN LAWRENCE *is sitting with him.*

Mix to:
Int. Day. Lobby, Officers' Mess

JOHN LAWRENCE *arrives and is met by* JEAN LAWRENCE.
JOHN: Where is he?

JEAN: In this awful hut. But the worst thing was that they didn't know anything about him, John.

JOHN: Didn't know he was coming?

JEAN: They knew he was coming, but they didn't know anything about him.

JOHN: (*To a physiotherapist,* MARK SMITH, *in a track suit*) Who is the Commanding Officer? Jean, you go back and wait with Robert. Keep him company. I'll sort this out.

MARK SMITH: This way, sir.

Int. Day. Nissen hut

ROBERT *is sitting slumped on the bed, a tired boy.* JEAN *puts an arm round him and sits with him again, waiting.*

Int. Day. Senior Medical Officer's office, rehabilitation unit

A GROUP CAPTAIN *shakes his head at* JOHN LAWRENCE.

GROUP CAPTAIN: Awful thing to say, but I don't know anything about your son, Wing Commander. Where is he?

Int. Day. Another office, rehabilitation unit

A SQUADRON LEADER *is sitting on the edge of a table with* DOCTORS, NURSES *of PMRAFNS, drinking coffee. The* GROUP CAPTAIN *comes in with* JOHN LAWRENCE.

GROUP CAPTAIN: This is Wing Commander Lawrence. He's come about his son, Squadron Leader Wentworth.

WENTWORTH: Do I know him?

JOHN: I don't know whether you know him or not, but you now know me, and I think you ought to get up from the edge of that table when introduced to a superior officer, even though retired, don't you?

Int. Day. Nissen hut

ROBERT'S *feet are being scratched with the end of a small hammer. When scratched, the toes on his left foot open instead of shutting. He is going through the tests again: eyes, reflexes, pins in his arm. Eyes closed, he has to touch his left arm with his right.* WENTWORTH *is doing the tests.*

WENTWORTH: Which finger am I holding?

ROBERT: Index. That's up. That's down.

　　(WENTWORTH *hasn't moved the finger.*)

WENTWORTH: Come on, Lawrence. Pay attention.

ROBERT: Bloody tests. You're always doing tests. Haven't you got my medical documents?

WENTWORTH: No, as a matter of fact we haven't.

ROBERT: Christ.

WENTWORTH: Your father gave me a lesson in military etiquette. I'll give you one. I'm called 'sir'.

ROBERT: What are you? Squadron Leader? In the Household Division we don't call your rank 'sir'.

WENTWORTH: Well, you can start now, Lawrence.

ROBERT: You're in the R.A.F. Are you a flyer?

WENTWORTH: No, I'm not. I'm a doctor.

ROBERT: Well, listen, doctor, test this fist. It's just about to give you your first fucking flying lesson!

Int. Day. Corridor, rehabilitation unit

SQUADRON LEADER WENTWORTH *comes out of the Nissen hut and nods to* JEAN LAWRENCE *as he goes past. She goes back in with* ROBERT.

Int. Day. Officers' Mess, rehabilitation unit

JOHN LAWRENCE *is brought in by the* GROUP CAPTAIN. *He turns round to go out again.*

JOHN: I don't want to come in here.

GROUP CAPTAIN: Please do, Wing Commander. I've sent for your wife . . .

JOHN: No. I want to be with my son.

(WENTWORTH, *coming in, is called over.*)

WENTWORTH: I've examined your son, Wing Commander, he's fine . . .

JOHN: *Fine!*

WENTWORTH: Considering the nature of his wound. I am more worried about his mental state.

JOHN: Are you? Well, I'm not.

GROUP CAPTAIN: You can take him away, you know. But you'll have to be responsible for him.

JOHN: I'm not afraid of that responsibility, I consider it an honour . . . I'll ask what he wants. (*His eyes fill with tears. He brushes his moustache.*) You don't deserve to know how brave that boy is.

Int. Day. Nissen hut

ROBERT *is listening to his father.* JEAN *is sitting with him.*

JOHN: They'll have to keep you here for a couple of weeks until they've assessed you. The Officers' Mess is a fire risk for serious cases, and you still are a serious case ... Do you want to come home?

ROBERT: No. I'll hack it.

JOHN: Well done, Spud.

JEAN: Do you want us to stay?

ROBERT: No.

JOHN: Right. I'll chase up Sophie.

ROBERT: No.

JOHN: She ought to have been to see you more. Perhaps she needs a lift ...

ROBERT: No, daddy, leave it. That's over.

    (JOHN *waits for a moment, looking at his son, then he kisses him and leaves.* JEAN *does the same.*)

Int. Day. Corridor, rehabilitation unit

JOHN LAWRENCE *waiting for his wife.*

JOHN: I'm not telling anybody any more about that boy, they don't deserve to know of his bravery.

Int. Day. Nissen hut

ROBERT *sitting on the bed. The* OLD MAN *coughs.*

ROBERT: What sort of car have you got?

OLD MAN: Eh?

Int. Day. Gym

Aerobics are in progress. ROBERT *is sitting on a horse at the back, watching.* MARK SMITH, *the physiotherapist, watching him.* ROBERT *is wearing his Sony Walkman. He is in a grey tracksuit.*

Mix to:
Int. Day. Gym

ROBERT *is lying on his back, his leg being stretched by* MARK SMITH. ROBERT *is screaming with the pain of it.*

MARK SMITH: Come on Robert, no need for that.

ROBERT: I don't mind pain. If I can scream, let me bloody scream. What sort of car do you drive?

MARK SMITH: A Cortina.

ROBERT: You would.

(ROBERT *kicks* MARK SMITH *with his right leg.*)

(*Shouts*) You do that again and I'll thump you!

Ext. Day. Rehabilitation unit

ROBERT *is walking, very slowly, from support to support, his Sony Walkman on his head.* SALLY, *a bright-eyed, plump physiotherapist, takes the earpiece out of one of his ears.*

SALLY: You're not supposed to have Walkmans. They don't help your balance.

ROBERT: They help mine, Sally.

(BOB, *a black-bearded civilian on crutches, dragging his feet, shouts across at* ROBERT.)

BOB: Hey, Robert! What you listening to? Captain Hook?

ROBERT: Billy Joel.

SALLY: I like Billy Joel.

BOB: Hey, Robert, come and sit over here. Keep away from those cripples. I hate cripples.

Int. Day. Rehabilitation unit

MARK SMITH *is putting ice into a bucket.* ROBERT, *with his left leg bare, looks at it in apprehension.* MARK SMITH *grins.*

MARK SMITH: Right ...

(*He shoves* ROBERT'S *left leg into the bucket of ice.* ROBERT *screams in agony.* MARK SMITH *pours in more ice.*)

Supposed to reduce the spasticity. Does it?

(BOB *swings over.*)

BOB: Hey, Robert, saying for the day: 'When you own a Lotus Super Seven, the world is your ashtray.' You dig?

Int. Day. Therapy workshop

SALLY *is trying hard to convince* ROBERT *that he ought to try woodwork. Baskets for weaving hang about the place. She has his hands up on a bench on a piece of wood that she wants him to sand, using both hands.*

SALLY: When you get good at it, you can go on and do all sorts of things — window boxes or even chairs, tables.

ROBERT: I'd much rather buy one, they're often quite good.

SALLY: Come on, Robert, that's not the point. Or you can do some visiting cards on the printing press ...

ROBERT: Rather not. Do you know how one goes about getting a disabled driver's sticker?

SALLY: Don't be silly.

ROBERT: Don't tell me not to be silly.

SALLY: Your income bracket is much too high for that.

ROBERT: For what?

SALLY: For a disabled driver's sticker.

ROBERT: How do I get one?

SALLY: I don't know.

ROBERT: It's nothing to do with income, you silly bitch. Don't you know anything about it? I want to drive my car. Why don't you know anything about it?

(ROBERT *is holding her wrist tightly with his right hand. The exertion is causing his left hand and arm to jerk in spasms.*)

SALLY: You're hurting my wrist.

ROBERT: You lot hurt me all the time. It's your job to know these things — why don't you? I knew how to do my job. We all did our jobs in the Falklands. Why can't you do your job?

(SALLY *pulls away from* ROBERT.)

To be honest, I don't think any of you know anything about us. You don't try to find out. You can't cope with us, can you? I don't know what it is I want, but it isn't window boxes, chairs, visiting cards printed badly. Oh, God! God!

(*He throws the piece of wood at* SALLY.)

Tell me how to get a disabled driver's sticker, you simpering wet cow!

(SALLY *goes, leaving* ROBERT *alone in the workshop except for an* OLDER MAN, *who is laboriously, tongue out, trying to thread a piece of plastic with a shoe lace.* ROBERT *flings the sander at him.*)

Int. Day. Kitchen of Stubbs house

GEORGE *is smiling and listening as* HUGH, *with the aid of cigarette packets and apples, shows the position of the Scots Guards on Tumbledown.*

HUGH: No, I was here with my platoon. You'd not gone far enough. The enemy here . . .

GEORGE: This is like the opening of *The Four Feathers*, except that was an old fogey . . . I suppose.

ROBERT: Yes.

HUGH: I'll tell you one thing, I didn't see any acts of bravery worth mentioning, except for Sergeant Brodick. I didn't see anything I could recommend, and that includes you, Peg.

(HUGH *gets up, throwing down the cigarette packet. He goes out.*)

HELEN: You're much more than friends, more like brothers.

ROBERT: Yes, we're very close.

Int. Day. Office, rehabilitation unit

A plain table. A barracks chair each side. Sitting at the table is an officer in combat dress with parachute wings and a major's rank. He has a file in front of him. The MAJOR *takes off his maroon beret, with its* RAMC *badge, and puts it on the table near the file. He is tough-looking, doesn't smile, doesn't invite warmth. There is a knock on the door and* ROBERT *comes in, the door held open for his wheelchair by* MARK SMITH.

ROBERT: Good morning.

MAJOR: Good morning.

ROBERT: Sorry about the wheelchair. I'm walking quite well now, but it has been a tiring morning with the sadists.

MAJOR: Sadists?

ROBERT: Physioterrorists.

MAJOR: Is that how you look at them?

ROBERT: I beg your pardon? I don't know your name.

MAJOR: Knox. RAMC. 5th Infantry Brigade. We wonder if you would care to answer a few questions . . . (*Opening the file*) . . . Robert. We're asking all the wounded for their impressions of the casualty evacuation, the whole thing, for a report. Would you care to?

ROBERT: What for?

MAJOR: So that next time we do it better.

ROBERT: Next time? All right, but you will have to answer some questions from me. Am I still going to be able to serve in the Army? What sort of pension can I expect if I'm discharged? How much of a disability pension can I expect? How much will I get from the South Atlantic Fund?

MAJOR: Hasn't anybody told you these things?

ROBERT: No. My father writes letters. He tries to find out. Nobody seems to know or wants to know.

MAJOR: All right, I'll try . . . But, first, name, rank and number . . . (*His pen is poised over the questionnaire.*)

ROBERT: Do you know, you're the first person I've seen in combat dress for months?

MAJOR: I'm sorry?

ROBERT: You must enjoy wearing it.

MAJOR: What is it like to kill?

Int. Day. Kitchen of Stubbs House

GEORGE STUBBS *is smiling at one end of the table.* ROBERT *is sitting alone at the other end.*

ROBERT: . . . The sort of questions you don't ask.

GEORGE: Why not? Don't you want to answer them?

ROBERT: Not very much.

GEORGE: Are you ashamed?

ROBERT: No, not at all. They weren't sixteen-year-old conscripts on Tumbledown, you know, starving or freezing or shot in the foot so that they couldn't run.

GEORGE: Weren't they?

ROBERT: No, they weren't. I'm not ashamed. You know, the strange thing is people treat me differently now. Young people ask my advice about their girlfriends, boyfriends. *Me.* I'm only twenty-three.

GEORGE: What about Hugh?

ROBERT: What about him?

GEORGE: Does he ask your advice?

ROBERT: Hugh is different.

GEORGE: Yes, he is, isn't he?

ROBERT: Where have they gone?

GEORGE: To talk, I suppose.

ROBERT: Hugh is jealous of me. He's always been jealous. You know, to be honest, Hugh was never a real soldier. He's cleverer than me in lots of ways, knows things, knows more, but he wasn't like me . . . He's jealous of my Military Cross, and he's jealous of the fact that I was a soldier through and through.

GEORGE: What was it like?

Int. Day. Office, rehabilitation unit

The MAJOR *is staring at* ROBERT *who is sweating and writhing in his wheelchair.*

ROBERT: They don't die.

MAJOR: How does it feel? Do you feel anything – elation, pleasure, sick?

ROBERT: You push the thing in and nothing happens. Mine broke off. I had to kill him with the broken end of it, stabbing and stabbing at him, and he was shouting at me, talking all the time, in Spanish, and I was stabbing him with my snapped-off bayonet, everywhere, in his face, his mouth, everywhere I could. He kept trying to hold it. He said 'please' in English.

MAJOR: What did it feel like?

ROBERT: When?

> (ROBERT *is very distressed. His leg is in spasm, and his arm is jerking wildly.*)

MAJOR: When he said 'please'?

ROBERT: It didn't feel like anything.

MAJOR: You didn't feel any ... sexual excitement?

ROBERT: No I didn't.

MAJOR: How many did you kill?

ROBERT: I don't know ...

Ext. Day. Rehabilitation unit

MARK SMITH *is running across the grass.* SALLY *waves to him from her workshop as she goes in.*

Int. Day. Therapy workshop

ROBERT, *in his wheelchair, is very distressed.* SALLY *cuddles him.* MARK SMITH *comes into the workshop.*

ROBERT: Who was he?

SALLY: I don't know.

MARK SMITH: I don't know. He just asked to see you.

ROBERT: He was very pushy, very pushy. (*Recovering, becoming angry*) Very, very pushy.

Int. Day. Kitchen of Stubbs house

Photographs of ROBERT's *head wound are laid out on the kitchen table for* GEORGE *to see.* ROBERT *takes another out of his wallet.*

GEORGE: Why do you carry them?

ROBERT: I don't know. To remind me of what they did to me? I know what I did to them. I sometimes think I should be affected. Everybody expects me to be. In a way, it's amazing that I am sane. And I am. The thing I hated most about it all ... You know talking to you – you're nobody: I know nothing about you, never will, you know more about me than I'll ever know about you, you're a blank sheet of paper – has made me think what it is. It isn't things like the nonsense of not being allowed on the Victory Parade, though I could have gone – to see it. I was invited by dear old Mappin and Webb to see it from their window and drink champagne. We should have been *in* it, in our wheelchairs, with our MOD minders. Not things like that at all, though pretty upsetting at the time. And there have been other things, the fuss over tiny things. Driving. Having to pay for my own tests to see if I could. Then my driving licence, getting it renewed. The whole driving thing, one day can, the next day can't. Oh, yes, all of that was bloody infuriating. I like driving. They said I could have fits. We had to go to three specialists before they would let me, and the Minister of Transport, the lot ... Nobody seemed to know how to cope with us.

GEORGE: I'm not surprised.

ROBERT: Don't let Helen see them. People faint.

GEORGE: Can *you* cope?

ROBERT: Now?

GEORGE: Yes.

Int. Day. Robert's flat

ROBERT *gets out of bed and dresses on his own, the whole business. When he has nearly finished, he goes into a spasm. He struggles to reach the telephone and manages to dial, then a voice at the other end can just be heard.* ROBERT *gasps into the telephone:*

ROBERT: Daddy, please come and help me.

Ext. Day. Railway bridge

ROBERT, *wearing a trilby, is walking slowly across the bridge. Behind him two running young* MEN *appear. They pass* ROBERT, *one of them taking his trilby and throwing it to the other.* ROBERT'S *head is shaven under the trilby.* ROBERT *shouts. The* MEN *come back and are joined by a* GIRL. *One of the* MEN *pushes* ROBERT *in the chest.* ROBERT *aims a blow at him and, because of his left leg, he falls. They kick him while he's on the ground, both the* MEN *and the* GIRL. *Their boots are aimed at* ROBERT'S *head.*

Ext. Day. Chelsea Barracks

A beautiful late-summer day. A GUARD OF HONOUR OF THE GRENADIER GUARDS *waits on the square.* ROBERT *is sitting alone by the gate, wearing a panama hat with the Brigade ribbon.*

Ext. Day. Embankment

Coaches full of SCOTS GUARDS *coming back from the Falklands are being driven along the Embankment.* HUGH MACKESSAC *is seen in one of them, his face at the window.* PETER FYSHE *is at another.*

Ext. Day. Chelsea Barracks

The GUARD OF HONOUR *is drawn up. The band is playing. All are at the far end of the barracks. The coaches are seen approaching.* ROBERT *gets to his feet and, as the first coach swings into the barracks, he raises his panama in salute. The coach shudders to a halt, and* BILL KIRKE *gets out, returning* ROBERT'S *salute, then hugging him.*

ROBERT: Welcome home, sir.

BILL KIRKE: How are you, Robert?

ROBERT: As you see, sir, on my feet. Glad you're back, sir. A lot of questions to ask.

BILL KIRKE: Well, we're back now.

> (BILL KIRKE *waves the coaches on and talks to* ROBERT *while the regiment is driven to its reception at the far end of the barracks.*)

Sit down. We can get on top of it for you. Please do sit down. You've been recommended for the Military Cross, you know. And you might as well know, you're pretty certain to get it.

ROBERT: Thank you, sir.

BILL KIRKE: I think the thing that has delighted me most is the fact that you have saluted me correctly while wearing a panama.

ROBERT: I looked it up, sir.

BILL KIRKE: They're expecting me the other end.

ROBERT: Yes, sir.

BILL KIRKE: Don't get up.

Ext. Day. The prow of a ship

ROBERT *is in the prow of the ship, moving from left to right this time, reflecting the movement of the ship. Music. The drums.*

Ext. Day. Chelsea Barracks

O'ROURKE, LUMPY *and* WATERSON *run across the barracks to* ROBERT. *They salute him, delighted.*

O'ROURKE: Come and meet the boys, sorr, the platoon, Sgt Brodick and all . . . Christ, it was awfu' down there. Dead boring.

(LUMPY *turns back to look for* SGT BRODICK.)

LUMPY: I'll tell him to keep the boys together.

WATERSON: Right . . .

(WATERSON *goes with him.* ROBERT *gets up and makes his way very slowly towards the far end, not making a very good job of it. After a few steps he realizes that* O'ROURKE *is not with him and looks back for him.* O'ROURKE *is standing stock-still. His hands make fists in his rage and sorrow.*)

ROBERT: What's wrong, Joe?

O'ROURKE: Fuck it! Why you? Of all the cunts in this battalion, why you?

(HUGH MACKESSAC *gets off the coach and walks towards* ROBERT.)

HUGH: Glorious weather, Bobbit. This the sort of weather you've been enjoying? It was appalling down there. You always manage to come off best!

Ext. Day. Garden of Stubbs house

HELEN *and* HUGH *are talking in the garden.*

HELEN: I don't think either of you will recover from it for a long time.

HUGH: I'm not envious of him, you know. He thinks I am, but not at all. How can I be envious of someone who has lost half his body?

Int. Day. Kitchen of Stubbs house

HUGH *comes into the kitchen to collect his cigarettes. In a sudden temper brought about by his thoughts and his walk from the garden, he shoves them into his pocket and strides out towards the car, calling:*

HUGH: Come on, Robert, we're off.

(ROBERT *gets to his feet, shaking his head, partly in amusement.*)

ROBERT: In lots of ways I don't think dear old Hugh knows what I've been through.

GEORGE: He should. He was there.

ROBERT: Yes, that's for sure, and . . . for ever. For us.

GEORGE: Helen has told him Louise isn't coming.

ROBERT: I think he guessed that.

GEORGE: Helen told her not to.

ROBERT: Oh, it would have been all right. Hugh is all right.

GEORGE: I'm sure. Yes. She wanted to make sure that my daughter didn't meet you.

ROBERT: Why?

GEORGE: We think she might find you as interesting as we do. She might have a penchant for killers, I suppose — one of the reasons she was attracted to Hugh. Goodness knows what she might do if she met a real one — by which I mean one who does not apologize.

ROBERT: Were you in the war, George?

GEORGE: Yes.

ROBERT: See any action?

GEORGE: No, I dug potatoes. I didn't agree with it all . . .

(GEORGE *laughs happily, freely, stimulated by* ROBERT's *grin.*)

ROBERT: What about all these things then, the prints, the medals, the badges?

GEORGE: Oh, I collect, but I don't *do*. Bit like the rest of the country.

ROBERT: You can't collect the smell.

GEORGE: No, I don't suppose so. Goodbye. Fascinating to have met you.

(HUGH *gets into the car.* ROBERT *goes out to it.* HELEN *joins* GEORGE.)

He's very angry.

HELEN: Isn't he?

GEORGE: They both are.

HELEN: Two killers. Two heroes?

74

GEORGE: We don't know yet, do we?

> (*They wave, as the car leaves with a roar and a scrunch of gravel.*)

I think it needed much more courage to do what he did than what I did.

HELEN: You mean fight?

GEORGE: No, I mean live.

> (*Music.*)

Ext. Day. Prow of the ship

ROBERT *is in the prow. The drums are rattling.*

Ext. Day. Approach to Mt Tumbledown

An O-group for platoon leaders of Right Flank Company, who are being briefed by PETER WALSH, *the company commander.* ROBERT *is scribbling in his notebook.*

PETER WALSH: Dress will be berets for the assault, steel helmets for reorganization. The pipes will be played on the enemy position tomorrow morning . . .

Mix to:
Ext. Night. Tumbledown sequence

The sequence is played to the music of the explosion of mines and grenades; the shouts and singing of the Argentinian soldiers of the 5th Battalion, the Naval Infantry Corps; the explosion of their mortar shells; the stutter of their machine-guns; the thud and explosion of 84-mm rocket launchers; the crack of sniper fire; the flare and bang of phosphorus grenades; small-arms fire, far off and near; the gunfire of ships at sea; the chatter of helicopters; the chatter of radios; the thud and explosion of 81-mm mortars; the noise of a single Bren gun; the shouts of the Argentinians in Spanish-American English and Spanish; their singing from their sangars up on the ridge of Tumbledown; their ten machine-guns on sustained fire, this din becoming louder and louder until it is the most terrifying and disorientating experience, numbing, threatening to turn all movement into stone, paralysing the will, emptying the body.

Over:
Ext. Night (last light). Mt Tumbledown

ROBERT *and his platoon move forward, his left section some paces to his front on the left, his right likewise on the right. He is in the centre with* LUMPY, *his wireless operator. Behind him is* SGT BRODICK *with the rear section. They stumble, slipping and sliding, over scree, difficult to walk over. There is no snow yet.*

Ext. Night. Mt Tumbledown

A rifle is stuck in the scree. A dead Scots Guardsman lies there. It is very eerie. ROBERT *and his platoon pass the dead man, looking back at him as they go on.*

Ext. Night. Mt Tumbledown

They move on through the scree. There is the sound of firing ahead. It is now the darkest it will be.

Ext. Night. Mt Tumbledown

PETER FYSHE *is sitting behind a rock, shivering, looking incredibly young. He hisses at* ROBERT *as he goes past*:

PETER FYSHE: Don't go on, Robert. It's awful. Don't let them make you. Shoot anyone who tries to make you . . .

> (ROBERT *glares at* PETER FYSHE, *who shuts up.* ROBERT *and his platoon go on.*)

Ext. Night. Left-flank position

ROBERT *and platoon are moving forward when an unidentified* VOICE *hisses out of the darkness*:

VOICE: For fuck's sake, get down, or you'll be hit.

> (ROBERT *goes down, together with his platoon. It is now half an hour before first light.* PAUL GREGORY *is seen on the right, by some rocks. He is looking very hard, efficient. He waves to* ROBERT *and talks to* PETER WALSH, *who has gone up to join him. Machine-gun fire comes from the summit. There are shouts and singing from the enemy positions.* SGT BRODICK *comes up to talk to* ROBERT.)

SGT BRODICK: Mr Fyshe back there, sorr, got caught in the back-blast of an 84-mm. Soon be out of it. He'll be fine.

ROBERT: Idiot!

> (*An 84-mm is fired at the enemy position. There is singing, and jeers as it misses.*)

They're supposed to run.

SGT BRODICK: Major Walsh, sorr . . .

> (SGT BRODICK *points out* PETER WALSH, *who is waving them up to him with* PAUL GREGORY.)

Ext. Night. Rocks

PETER WALSH *briefs his platoon commanders,* ROBERT, HUGH, *the* NOBLE LORD, *with* PAUL GREGORY *near.*

PETER WALSH: One machine-gun post, possibly more. Number One platoon will join Left Flank here in extended line to act as a fire base. Robert, Hugh, Two and Three platoons will do a right-flank attack on the MG post, going down the gully which runs down the right-hand side of Tumbledown crags. Can you see it?

> (PAUL GREGORY *points it out to* HUGH *and* ROBERT.)

Three to be left-hand assault platoon. Two to be right-hand assault platoon . . .

ROBERT: Peter?

PETER WALSH: Robert.

ROBERT: We know what's to the front. We don't know what's behind. I'm senior. I should take the right hand.

PETER WALSH: Yes, all right.

Ext. Night. Left-flank position

ROBERT'S SECTION COMMANDERS, *with* SGT BRODICK, *are waiting. They watch* ROBERT *come back. He briefs them. They go back to their sections and move to the right of the rocks towards the gully.*

Ext. Night. Gully

ROBERT *and his platoon move up the gully first, followed by* HUGH *and his platoon. One platoon forms the fire base.* LUMPY *is with* ROBERT.

Ext. Night. Ahead

ARGENTINIAN SOLDIERS *are seen moving across the front in file.* ROBERT *takes* LUMPY'S *rifle, which has an individual weapon sight and shoots at them, dropping a few.*

ROBERT: Look, targets fall when hit!

> (ROBERT *carries on along the gully.* LUMPY *is with him.*)

Lumpy, call One and ask for fire on the MG post, otherwise we'll miss it . . .

Ext. Night. Gully

LUMPY: Hello, One-one, this is One-three. Over.

ONE: One-one, send. Over.

LUMPY: One-three, bring fire to bear on enemy. Over.

ONE: One-one, wilco. Out.

> (*Fire from* ONE PLATOON *shows where the machine-gun post is.* ROBERT *is dead-centre on it in the gully.*)

ROBERT: All right, come on, let's go!

> (ROBERT *gets up and goes without looking back. The whole platoon is up and with him,* PROTHERO *firing his general-purpose machine-gun from his hip. Rocket launchers are fired, both 84-mm and 66-mm. There are ricochets from the rocks ahead and machine-gun fire from the enemy position. The* ARGENTINIANS *are singing and shouting as they put down fire. There are ricochets everywhere.* THREE PLATOON *goes down.*)

Ext. Night. Ground in front of machine-gun position

ROBERT, *with his platoon, fires at the machine-gun position, but so much is coming back at them that they realize they won't win the fire fight.* ROBERT *crawls forward with a white phosphorus grenade, trying to pull the pin out. It won't come out. He almost reaches the machine-gun position. The pin is bent back and he can't budge it. He crawls back to* CPL BAYNES.

ROBERT: Can't get the pin out. Here, Corporal Baynes, you pull. I'll hold the grenade.

> (*Intense fire is raining down on them.* ROBERT *crawls on up with the pin out this time.*)

Ext. Night. Large rock

The most fearful machine-gun fire is coming down from more than one position. There is singing, shouting. ROBERT *is behind the rock. He shits himself. Fire from his own platoon is coming at him also.*

ROBERT: (*Screams*) For fuck's sake, reduce fire!

> (*He stands up and throws the grenade. Then, still standing, after a small tussle with the next pin, he throws another.*)

Come on, boys!

> (ROBERT *runs the next few metres, firing as he goes.* PROTHERO *and the rest of the platoon run with him.* PROTHERO *catches up with*

ROBERT, *firing his machine-gun from the hip and socking rounds into the machine-gun position.*)

Ext. Night. Machine-gun position

An ARGENTINIAN SOLDIER, *with hands up, is grabbed by* ROBERT, *who holds him with his left hand, rifle in his right, neither of them knowing what to do (the nightmare on the ship).* ROBERT's *platoon is with him. The* PRISONERS *are pushed to the ground.* ROBERT *jumps into a trench, where there is a dead* ARGENTINIAN. ROBERT *pulls his head back by the hair, then searches him for his pistol and shoves it down the front of his smock.* ROBERT's *equipment and webbing and parts of his smock are now in shreds. Fire is still coming from somewhere. Now it is first light. The position has been taken.* THREE PLATOON *are enjoying the* PRISONERS, *the first Argentinians they have seen.* SGT BRODICK *grips them, as does* ROBERT.

ROBERT: Stop playing with them. We're still being fired on.

(SGT BRODICK *takes off his webbing, hands his rifle to one of the platoon, pulls the pin from a grenade with difficulty and scrambles forward to deal with one of the next two machine-gun positions.*)

SGT BRODICK: You, Pongo, up there! Lumpy, come on!

Ext. Day. Large rock

ROBERT, PROTHERO *and* LUMPY *scuttle around the rock. As they do so everything seems to come at them; everything explodes with fire. They scuttle back.* PROTHERO *looks up. Argentinian shouts and singing can be heard. The air is exploding with sustained fire.* PROTHERO *climbs the rock, up and up. Then he is shot in the thigh and in the stomach.* ROBERT *sees him fall and grabs two* GUARDSMEN *and* FRASER. *They skirmish to the right.*

Ext. Day. Grassy stretch

They advance across the grass in pairs in exemplary fashion, as if on a close-combat range, expecting targets to pop up. They do. They are shot at. They go down. ROBERT *passes a* MAN *lying face-down. He runs forward and then goes back to look at the* MAN, *wondering if he is dead.* ROBERT *sticks his bayonet into the* MAN's *arm. He is still alive and turns over, screaming. The bayonet snaps off.* ROBERT *stabs at the* MAN *with the broken bayonet, the* MAN *trying hard to fend him off.* ROBERT *shoots him, clubs him, stabs the stub of his bayonet into him, again and again. The* MAN *shouts and screams. Among all the shouting we hear 'Please'. He is finally dead.* ROBERT *is exuberant. He plucks up the* MAN's *FN rifle. He now has one in each hand and skirmishes forward in a pair with* FRASER, *greatly elated.*

Ext. Day. Prow of the ship

For the first time ROBERT *laughs, his hair blowing in the wind as the ship streams on, at the whole seductive wonder of it. Music.*

Ext. Day. Summit, Mt Tumbledown

ROBERT *and* FRASER *are climbing, the other two ahead of them.* FRASER *stops and tugs at* ROBERT's *sleeve.*

FRASER: Excuse me, sorr, I think I've been hit . . .

   (ROBERT *grins wildly at him. His grin says that surely* FRASER *must know if he's been hit and they must get on because the music is playing and the blood is up. With very slow movements* FRASER *turns to show him the wound from behind.*)

Ext. Day. View from the summit

ROBERT *sees the way ahead: the port of Stanley, a ship in the harbour.*

ROBERT: There it is, and Hugh will be behind, sweeping . . . And there it is!

   (*He takes three very slow steps forward, the last three real steps he will ever take. He is delighted.*)

Isn't this fun?

   (*A great blow to the back of his head stuns him, and he starts to go down.*)

Ext. Day. Mt Tumbledown, 14 June 1982

Sky. The sound of a helicopter. Flurries of snow. The sound of wind in the crags.

Ext. Day. Chelsea Barracks

The panama hat of ROBERT LAWRENCE *is raised in salute.*